St. Ninian's Parish Church
Library

PERSONAL VICTORY

D0785503

PERSONAL VICTORY

Colin Urquhart

HODDER AND STOUGHTON
LONDON SYDNEY AUCKLAND TORONTO

Biblical quotations are from the New International Version

British Library Cataloguing in Publication Data

Urquhart, Colin
  Personal victory.
  1. Christian life
  I. Title
  248.4

  ISBN 0 340 48501 9

*Copyright © 1988 by Colin Urquhart. First printed 1988. All rights
reserved. No part of this publication may be reproduced or transmitted in
any form or by any means, electronically or mechanically, including
photocopying, recording or any information storage or retrieval system,
without either prior permission in writing from the publisher or a licence,
permitting restricted copying. In the United Kingdom such licences are
issued by the Copyright Licensing Agency, 33–34 Alfred Place, London
WC1E 7DP. Printed in Great Britain for Hodder and Stoughton Limited,
Mill Road, Dunton Green, Sevenoaks, Kent TN13 2YA by Cox & Wyman
Ltd., Reading, Berks. Typeset by Hewer Text Composition Services,
Edinburgh. Hodder and Stoughton Editorial Office: 47 Bedford Square,
London WC1B 3DP.*

To all those who want to live
a victorious Christian life

Contents

Acknowledgments

My thanks to all who have worked with me in the preparation of this book, especially to Rose-Mary who has laboured diligently on the word processor and has assisted in preparing the material for publication. She has been helped by Alison and Heather.

I am also thankful to all at Kingdom Faith Ministries for their love, prayer and encouragement.

My wife and daughter, Andrea, have been able to rejoice that I could be based at home while writing; a real treat for all of us!

My prayer is that the Lord Jesus will use this little book to point the way to a victorious Christian life for many who have found the way difficult.

C.U.

1

Living in Victory

The way to victory:
God's purpose is for you to live in personal victory.
This is possible by faith in Jesus who has *already*
overcome the world and is reigning in triumph.

Your victory scripture:
Without faith it is impossible to please God. (Heb. 11:6)

Many Christians find it difficult to believe they can live in victory! Yet God's purpose is for them to overcome their difficulties, not be defeated by them.

Jesus does not promise His followers an easy life. Neither does He offer trite answers to people's needs. Instead He makes it clear that God's power and resources are available to those who believe in Him.

Those who appropriate these resources will be victorious. They will overcome their problems through faith in Jesus Christ. **This is possible for you because it is God's will for you**.

He has not called you to be defeated or to fail. **He has called you to a life of victorious faith**.

THE LORD'S PURPOSE

Faith overcomes the world

Christians talk about the victory of the Cross, the resurrection and the ultimate victory of Jesus when He comes again

11

in glory. Why do they hesitate to speak of living in personal victory? Is this because of unbelief? Do they have the kind of faith which believes the right doctrines, but makes little difference to their daily lives?

'This is the victory that has overcome the world, even our faith,' says John (1 John 5:4).

Men and women of faith will live in victory. They *have* overcome the world. 'Who is it that overcomes the world? Only he who believes that Jesus is the Son of God' (1 John 5:5). **If you believe Jesus is the Son of God you can overcome whatever problems confront you**. God has already given you a faith which overcomes. Jesus is greater than any problem or need. He proclaimed boldly, 'I have overcome the world' (John 16:33).

As He has overcome the world so He anticipates that those who believe in Him will overcome.

Paul was a realist, as well as a man of great faith. He faced many seemingly impossible situations, and suffered both rejection and frequent physical punishment for the sake of the gospel. Yet he could say:

We are hard pressed on every side, but not crushed; perplexed, but not in despair; persecuted, but not abandoned; struck down, but not destroyed. (2 Cor. 4:8–9)

He maintained this positive attitude because, although he lived with a constant awareness of his own weakness, he knew the treasure of God's 'all surpassing power' within him.

As a Christian **you have this same power within you; you have the person of God Himself, the Holy Spirit, living in you; you have Christ in you.**

And it is His purpose to lead you in His triumphant procession.

It is not by determination nor your own strength that you will triumph; but by faith in Jesus working within you through His Spirit.

IF YOU TRUST IN YOURSELF, YOU WILL FAIL;
IF YOU TRUST IN HIM, HE WILL ENABLE YOU
TO OVERCOME.
**God does not want you to fail; He wants you to be
victorious.**

REWARDS OF FAITH

Great promises are given to those who overcome. To them
God 'will give the right to eat from the tree of life, which is
in the paradise of God' (Rev. 2:7). They will not be hurt in
any way by the second death and their names will never be
erased from the book of life. Jesus will acknowledge them
before His Father and His angels. They will be given the
right to sit with Jesus on His throne, just as Jesus overcame
and sat down with His Father on His throne.

**These wonderful promises are for you. This is God's will
and purpose for you. He wants you to overcome, to live in
victory and triumph through Jesus Christ. He wants you
reigning with Him in glory.**

First you need to learn to reign in this life through faith.
For 'without faith it is impossible to please God, because
anyone who comes to him must believe that he exists and
that he rewards those who earnestly seek him' (Heb. 11:6).

As a Christian how can you overcome the world, the
flesh and the devil? How can you live in the victory Jesus
has won for you on the cross and demonstrated in His
resurrection? How can you be victorious in prayer, believing God's promises and seeing them fulfilled? How can you
know victory in the conflicts within you and the difficult
circumstances around you?

CONCENTRATION ON PROBLEMS

Many Christians make the fatal mistake of concentrating
on the problem instead of the answer. To speak of victory

is unrealistic, they suggest. Instead they speak endlessly of their needs, difficulties and sicknesses.

Isn't this a great temptation? It is so easy to spend your prayer time thinking about your problems, instead of expecting Jesus to deal with them. It is tempting to keep telling others about your difficulties because you want them to understand your situation or feel sorry for you. It seems so natural, and yet such conversations can seriously hinder faith.

How different this is from the way Jesus taught His disciples to live! **For Jesus, faith is the only realistic way of living**. Faith in God's love. Faith in God's power. Faith in God's mercy and grace.

Jesus said: 'Come to me, all you who are weary and burdened, and I will give you rest' (Matt. 11:28). I was taught to do this every time I prayed and it was impressed on me that it did not take long to pass a burden over, once I was prepared to let go of it.

You do not have to go into an immense amount of detail; the Lord knows more about your situation than you do. It is like handing the burden of a full suitcase to someone else. You do not set the case on the ground, open it and describe all its contents. If somebody offers to carry the burden, you simply hand over the suitcase, together with everything in it.

And you do not keep hold of one corner when you hand the burden to Jesus. He is able to carry the entire weight.

This is one of the first elementary acts of faith for you to learn. **Jesus loves you so much He wants to carry your burdens**.

He encouraged His disciples to live in faith, and His greatest disappointments over them were on the occasions when they failed to exercise that faith: 'O unbelieving and perverse generation, how long shall I stay with you? How long shall I put up with you?' (Matt. 17:17).

Many situations will challenge your faith. Jesus was not afraid to confront problems. He teaches that anyone who speaks to a mountain of need in faith, will see that mountain moved if he 'believes that what he says will happen' (Mark 11:23). Jesus says this of 'anyone', **and that includes you!**

You do not please the Lord by carrying burdens He wants to lift from you. He is honoured, not by the passive acceptance of problems, but by the faith which confronts and overcomes them.

You will live in victory if you live by the principles of faith Jesus taught.

Faith in Jesus trusts Him instead of self.
Faith in Jesus believes Him to change the circumstances instead of submitting to problems.
Faith in Jesus believes what He says, instead of doubting His Word.
Faith in Jesus acts on the Word instead of being dis-obedient.

You may love the Lord Jesus sincerely and desire earnestly to be true to Him, and yet still experience much failure and frustration.

God confronts all of us with our shortcomings, including those of faith, only that He might teach us to trust Him more fully. He wants to teach you to be victorious in your daily life.

This is to become your experience, not simply a pious hope. **Jesus wants you to overcome your circumstances not to be overcome by them. He does not want you to be the victim; but the victor. He does not want you to be trampled underfoot; He wants you to triumph!**

Your key to a victorious life:
FAITH IN JESUS ENABLES YOU TO OVER-COME.

2

The Victory of the Cross

The way to victory:
   The victory of the Cross over every human need and every spiritual power is available to *you* through faith.

Your victory scripture:
   The message of the cross is foolishness to those who are perishing, but to us who are being saved it is the power of God. (1 Cor. 1:18)

To live by faith is to live in the victory Jesus has already won for you on the Cross.

During His pastoral ministry Jesus overcame sin, sickness and even death. What He did then has been made available to those of any generation who put their faith in Him. The Cross has eternal value for every believer.

Death is God's just and holy judgment on sin. Because He never sinned, Jesus did not deserve to die. He fulfilled completely His Father's will, being obedient to Him in every way, regardless of the cost.

He offered His life as a sacrifice on behalf of sinners. All who grieve the Lord by their sins can know His forgiveness and complete deliverance from guilt. Jesus also took upon Himself all the suffering, affliction and rejection we can experience. He was even oppressed and 'crushed' for us, experiencing complete dereliction on the Cross: 'My God, my God, why have you forsaken me?'

At that moment, Jesus was totally identified with the needs of every human being. He knew the separation from the Father which is the direct consequence of sin, not His own sin, but yours and mine.

IT IS DONE

There was nothing sentimental about the Cross. Jesus bore on His body the marks of betrayal and severe disfigurement, caused by the torture to which He was subjected. As He hung there He was without any beauty or attraction, despised, rejected and hated.

This was the cost of giving His sinless life as an offering for sinners, His righteous life for the unrighteous, His perfect life for the imperfect, His obedient life for the disobedient, His successful life on behalf of failures. All who have sinned can find their identity in Christ on the Cross. He died for all.

The disfigured, the ordinary, the despised, the rejected, the oppressed, all had their needs met by Jesus at that moment. He experienced oppression from the devil, religious leaders, temporal authorities and through physical suffering. Yet He emerged triumphant.

God's love for you took Jesus to the Cross, so you might be set free from sin, oppression, rejection, sickness and every other need. Because of what He suffered He is able to lead you through the difficulty to a place of victory.

Like you, I am often aware of my total unworthiness before God. I wonder how He could have chosen me out of the mass of humanity, to be His child. It seems inconceivable that the Holy God should want to have anything to do with me in any way. He must be aware of my ungodly thoughts and desires. And how I must hurt Him every time I sin or disobey His Word.

And yet I have had to come to terms with the truth. In

Jesus, He has demonstrated His love for me. **The Cross is personal for *me*. Jesus died for *me*.** And when I ask Him to forgive my sins, His blood cleanses me from all that is unholy in His sight. He makes me worthy in God's Presence. I can stand before His throne clothed in the white garment of righteousness which He puts on me.

I deserve none of this. It is the work of His grace. And what He has done for me, He has done for you.

As Jesus triumphed on the Cross, you can triumph in faith as you appropriate what He did for you there.

THE MESSAGE OF THE CROSS

Jesus warned His followers they would have trouble in this life, but reminded them He had overcome the world. He promised to be with them always. No matter what their difficulties, He would never leave them. His physical presence with them would give way to His living presence within them through the Holy Spirit. And He promised to answer their prayers of faith. Whatever they ask in His name will be given to them – if they believe!

Paul recognises, 'The message of the cross is foolishness to those who are perishing, but to us who are being saved it is the power of God' (1 Cor. 1:18). **The Cross is the power which enables you to overcome. For Jesus met your need there. He did everything necessary:**

> **to ensure forgiveness of your sins,**
> **to free you from every spiritual bondage,**
> **to make possible the healing of any emotional or physical need.**

No wonder Paul said: 'For I resolved to know nothing while I was with you except Jesus Christ and him crucified' (1 Cor. 2:2).

Paul testified: 'I have been crucified with Christ and I no

longer live, but Christ lives in me. The life I live in the body, I live by faith in the Son of God, who loved me and gave himself for me' (Gal. 2:20). At the time of the crucifixion Paul was Jesus' enemy. He came to realise that the old Saul of Tarsus with all his pride and misplaced religious and legalistic fervour, was put to death on the Cross, so that a new man could be brought to life, Paul the apostle. He became a man of faith, because he understood **he could only receive this new life through faith in Jesus crucified, and he could only live the new life by continuing to live by faith.**

THE EXTENT OF THE VICTORY

The Cross marked the beginning of a new covenant, a new relationship, between God and men. It marked the end of trying to please God by formal, religious observances, and heralded a new era of faith.

When you surrendered your life to the Lordship of Jesus:

> God made you alive with Christ. He forgave us all our sins, having cancelled the written code, with its regula-tions, that was against us and that stood opposed to us; he took it away, nailing it to the cross. (Col. 2:13–14)

The law gives way to faith in Jesus. **Now by faith you can share in His triumph.**

This victory not only meets every human need; it is also the means by which all the spiritual powers of darkness are overcome:

> And having disarmed the powers and authorities, he made a public spectacle of them, triumphing over them by the cross. (Col. 2:15)

All your needs have been met in the crucified Jesus. He is now risen in triumph. And the promise of God's Word to you is this: 'And my God will meet all your needs according to his glorious riches in Christ Jesus.' (Phil. 4:19). **These glorious riches are yours in Christ Jesus.**

In Him your old life is crucified.
In Him you are raised to a new life.
In Him your needs are met.
In Him you can triumph.

Your key to a victorious life:
ALL YOUR NEEDS HAVE BEEN MET IN THE CRUCIFIED JESUS.

3

Victory in the Name of Jesus

The way to victory:
   Jesus' name has power and authority over everything
   material and spiritual. You will not fail if you do things
   in His name.

Your victory scripture:
   And whatever you do, whether in word or deed, do it all
   in the name of the Lord Jesus. (Col. 3:17)

Jesus was victorious on the Cross, overcoming sin, sickness
and every form of evil. His name is above every other
name. He is supreme. He is Lord.

   Therefore God exalted him to the highest place and gave
   him the name that is above every name, that at the name
   of Jesus every knee should bow, in heaven and on earth
   and under the earth, and every tongue confess that Jesus
   Christ is Lord, to the glory of God the Father. (Phil.
   2:9–11)

THE NAME THAT SAVES

The Father exalted Jesus because of His perfect obedience
in fulfilling His purpose on earth. Now His name is above
every name in heaven and earth. He has power and
authority over everything spiritual or material. 'He became

as much superior to the angels as the name he has inherited
is superior to theirs' (Heb. 1:4).

In scripture the name denotes the person. The name of
Jesus signifies all that He is and everything He has done.
You cannot separate the name of Jesus either from the
words He spoke, or from the things He accomplished.

Jesus is the Way, the Truth and the Life. There is no
other way to heaven except through Jesus. There is no
other name by which a man can be saved, 'Salvation is
found in no-one else, for there is no other name under
heaven given to men by which we must be saved' (Acts
4:12). It is by the power of the name of the crucified and
victorious Jesus that **you have been accepted and forgiven
by God. Through Him you have received new life and the
gift of God's Kingdom.**

If you confess with your mouth, 'Jesus is Lord,' and
believe in your heart that God raised him from the dead,
you will be saved. (Rom. 10:9)

Jesus is the name of salvation. Salvation means healing
and deliverance. So this is the name by which you can know
victory in every circumstance of your life.
Through Jesus you have been:

saved from sin;
saved from sickness and rejection;
saved from poverty and despair;
saved from Satan and the powers of darkness;
**saved from the curse of the law and the demands of
    legalistic religion;**
**saved from yourself and your complete helplessness
    without a Saviour.**

EVERYTHING IN HIS NAME

No wonder you are encouraged to do everything in the
name of Jesus! **'And whatever you do, whether in word or**

**deed, do it all in the name of the Lord Jesus, giving thanks to
God the Father through him'** (Col. 3:17).

It brought a revolution in my own life and ministry to
realise that I was called by God to do everything in the
name of Jesus. At first it seemed a daunting prospect. How
could I possibly live up to such a high calling? Then I began
to see something of the principle of speaking on Jesus'
behalf, and being invited to pray what He would pray.

Would the Father really listen to me as He listens to His
Son? Then came the recognition that God has made me a
son and has put His own name upon me. I was not to waste
the privilege the Lord had given me.

The more I dared to believe, the more He would do. The
more bold I became in faith, the greater the faith God could
honour. The more I understood that I am in Christ and He
in me, the more thankful I became that He both heard and
answered me.

My first steps in faith seemed tentative, and yet God
honoured them. Answers to prayer are a great encouragement!

I learnt to thank the Lord for allowing me to fail at times,
for then I had trusted in myself and not in Him. I had
viewed my situation through purely human eyes, without
the perspective that Jesus would bring.

Slowly I began to make more use of the privilege of
praying in His name. 'If this is how Jesus would view the
situation, then this is how I will view it. If that is what He
would pray, that is what I will pray.'

Often I had to admit I did not believe what He would
believe, or expect the answers He anticipated. But as I
humbled myself before the Lord, confessing my unbelief,
so then I could receive the words of faith with which He
wanted to encourage me.

It is inconceivable that Jesus should ever fail. If you act in
His name you act on His behalf, saying or doing what He
would say or do in that situation. You will look at your
circumstances through His eyes, praying what He would

pray, believing what He would believe. Like Him, you have available to you the riches and resources of heaven.

When you act in your own strength, or do what is opposed to God's purpose, you will experience failure, frustration and defeat. You have to acknowledge the far-reaching power that faith releases into your life.

> I tell you the truth, if you have faith as small as a mustard seed, you can say to this mountain, 'Move from here to there' and it will move. Nothing will be impossible for you. (Matt. 17:20)

NOTHING WILL BE IMPOSSIBLE FOR YOU. This is the result of faith working in your life. Again Jesus affirms: **'Everything is possible for him who believes'** (Mark 9:23).

PRAY IN HIS NAME

Every time you say the Lord's Prayer you acknowledge that God's holy name is to be praised. And Jesus makes a series of amazing promises of what God will do when you pray in His name:

> And I will do whatever you ask in my name, so that the Son may bring glory to the Father. You may ask me for anything in my name, and I will do it. (John 14:13–14)

> You did not choose me, but I chose you and appointed you to go and bear fruit – fruit that will last. Then the Father will give you whatever you ask in my name. (John 15:16)

> I tell you the truth, my Father will give you whatever you ask in my name. (John 16:23)

What a privilege to be invited by Jesus to use His name in prayer as a guarantee you will be heard and answered! What a privilege to be given such wonderful promises by the One who has never broken His word! What encouragement to learn how to pray in the name of Jesus!

But He makes it clear that the one who truly prays in His name, will not pray with doubt, or be double-minded about the outcome. He will believe he has received the answer.

> **You are saved by the name of Jesus.**
> **You can act in the name of Jesus.**
> **You can speak in the name of Jesus.**
> **You are to pray in the name of Jesus.**
> **You have authority through the name of Jesus.**
> **You have power in the name of Jesus.**
> **You can heal in the name of Jesus.**
> **You are protected by the name of Jesus.**

All this because: **You have faith in the name of Jesus.**

This is your calling as a child of God, and we shall see how you can fulfil such a calling. Understand that this is possible for you. Because you are saved by His name, you can say and do everything in His name, on His behalf, expecting victory.

Before going to the Cross Jesus prayed that the disciples would be protected by the power of His name:

Holy Father, protect them by the power of your name – the name you gave me – so that they may be one as we are one. While I was with them, I protected them and kept them safe by that name you gave me. (John 17:11–12)

That same protection is yours because you belong to Jesus. You are protected by the power of His name, as you seek to walk in faithful and loving obedience to His word.

BY FAITH IN THE NAME OF JESUS

After the resurrection and the coming of the Holy Spirit at Pentecost, the disciples saw the fruit of acting in the name

of Jesus. When Peter and John healed the crippled beggar
at the gate of the temple, they told the crowd:

> By faith in the name of Jesus, this man whom you see and
> know was made strong. It is Jesus' name and the faith
> that comes through him that has given this complete
> healing to him, as you can all see. (Acts 3:16)

When later they had to give an account to the Jewish
council as to why the man had been healed, the High Priest
asked them, 'By what power or what name did you do this?'
The answer that Peter gave reiterated what he and John
had told the crowd, 'It is by the name of Jesus Christ of
Nazareth, whom you crucified but whom God raised from
the dead, that this man stands before you healed' (Acts
4:10).

Is the name of Jesus as powerful now as then? Of course.
Is faith in His name the same? That is the crucial question.
Where such faith exists people today are healed in the
name of Jesus, and their needs are met.

The name of Jesus brings salvation. Everything is
possible to those who believe in Him. His name protects all
who belong to Him. By His name the sick are healed and
those in bondage are set free. The name of Jesus is above
every other name in heaven or on earth.

**As you learn to speak out and pray in His name, you will
experience personal victory.**

Your key to a victorious life:
  THE WAY OF VICTORY IS TO SPEAK, ACT AND
  PRAY IN THE NAME OF JESUS.

4

Victory in the Holy Spirit

The way to victory:
> You can experience victory by submitting your human spirit to the Holy Spirit. He will lead you into victory, not failure and defeat.

Your victory scripture:
> The Spirit gives life; the flesh counts for nothing. (John 6:63)

GOD'S PLAN FOR YOUR LIFE

Jesus has been victorious on the Cross. In His name you can be victorious. Now you need to see how this victory can be applied to your life. Paul prays:

> May your whole spirit, soul and body be kept blameless at the coming of our Lord Jesus Christ. The one who calls you is faithful and he will do it. (1 Thess. 5:23–24)

The Lord wants you to live in faith and victory. His purpose is to sanctify you, to make you holy, like Jesus in spirit, soul and body. These are not two separate purposes, but different parts of one overall plan He has for your life:

He wants you to live by faith in Jesus.
He wants you to live in victory.
He wants you to live in love for God and others – faith working through love.

**He wants to sanctify you in spirit, soul and body, making
you holy like Jesus.**
He wants to keep you blameless in His sight.

This is God's plan for every Christian. He calls us to
different ministries, but all within the same plan. To see
how this plan will be effected in your own life, it is
important to understand the different functions of your
spirit, soul and body.

BEFORE YOUR NEW BIRTH

Before you became a Christian you lived 'according to the
flesh', your soul and body acting independently of God.
　The soul consists of three main areas:

a)　the mind, including your reason and intellect
b)　the emotions or feelings
c)　the will, your ability to make decisions and choices.

Before you were a Christian you had your own ideas about
everything, including God. These ideas formed the foundation of what you believed as a person, and therefore
influenced the way you chose to act. There may have been
no reference to God at all in your thinking even though you
might have believed in His existence. Or you may have
attended some form of worship, but without enjoying a
personal relationship with Jesus. Until your new birth,
your mind was not submitted to the Spirit of God and could
not be informed by Him as to His will and purpose.
　The different functions of the soul interrelate and
influence one another. So, for example, whatever goes on
in the mind influences the emotions. If someone thinks
negatively about himself, he will feel negative and make
negative decisions with his will. Then his behaviour will be
negative.
　Before your new birth you probably lived on your
feelings to a great extent. You did what you felt like doing,

and tried to avoid what you did not want to do. You were the victim of the way in which others spoke to you and treated you. You may have harboured feelings of bitterness, resentment and hurt. You may have lived an immoral life seeking the fulfilment of your fleshly desires. You may have been involved in dubious business practices. You may have tried to live a 'good' life, but with very independent attitudes.

Because your mind was conditioned by your own ideas and way of thinking, and because your life was influenced greatly by your feelings, you used your will to please yourself, or to do what you thought right according to your own wisdom. You acted independently of any direction from God.

This is the way that most people live. However it is not the way God intends His children to behave.

THE NEW BIRTH CHANGES THINGS

When you were born again you became a Christian through your faith in Jesus Christ. At that point something dynamic happened in your human spirit. The Spirit of God came into your spirit and brought you to life spiritually. Before your new birth you had a human spirit, but it was to all intents and purposes dead. It did not influence your life in a positive direction. You lived a soulish, rather than a spiritual life.

Jesus said, 'God is spirit, and his worshippers must worship in spirit and in truth' (John 4:24). God communicates with you spiritually. You can hear His voice and receive revelation from Him in your spirit rather than in your mind.

With your mind you can appreciate and understand what God has said to you. But it is in your spirit you receive revelation. There are several ways in which this can happen. Often it occurs as you read the Bible. It can also take place when reading a spiritual book, listening to a sermon or in conversation. Suddenly something lights up inside you and you know you have heard the Lord.

So when you came alive spiritually, God could begin to produce in you His order for your life. The Holy Spirit could work through your human spirit to influence your soul.

THE SOUL AND SPIRIT

The Lord wants your mind to be submitted to His thinking.
The Lord wants your feelings ruled by His Spirit.
The Lord wants your will submitted to His will.

If your soul is submitted to the Lord, His Spirit is able to flow out of your body like rivers of living water. This is how Jesus described the activity of His Spirit in believers.

In the Figure the diagram on the left describes this process:

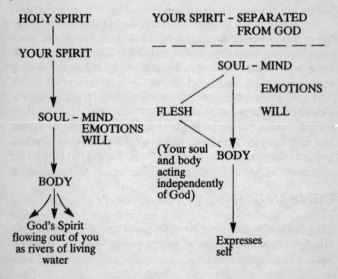

This submission does not come easily to any of us. We often want our own way. We want to receive God's blessings and live in obedience to Him, but without too much cost. We can feel aggressive about our own views. We want to impress others with our knowledge. It matters immensely how we feel about things, and we expect others to be considerate about our feelings.

We think it sufficient to desire God's will, but without doing it. We are quick to notice others' faults and failings, but expect them to be gracious, forgiving and understanding about our own inadequacies. We certainly do not readily view others the way we want them to view us.

Submission does not come naturally or easily, but it is vitally necessary if we are to see God glorified in our lives.

The Holy Spirit cannot direct your body without the willing co-operation of the soul. When the soul is submitted to the Spirit, you can express the new life in your body. Without this co-operation you will act according to your natural inclinations and senses, and inevitably grieve the Lord.

The term 'flesh' in the New Testament does not refer to the physical body alone, but to the way in which the soul and the body act independently of God. This is the way you lived before your new birth, but it is not how you are to live now.

If you raise your soul above the Spirit by choosing to please yourself rather than the Lord, the result is a crushed spirit. Your spirit feels weighed down. God has not taken His Spirit away from you, but He cannot function within you, or express His life through you, in the way He desires.

GOD'S ORDER

This is God's order for your life: your soul submitted to His Spirit, so that rivers of living water flow out of your life.

Your mind submitted to the Spirit, **which means you live according to God's Word.** Your thinking is informed by His truth revealed in the scriptures.

Your emotions submitted to God's Spirit. Because you want to please Him, *you do not allow your feelings to rule you; you allow the Spirit to rule your feelings*. You will not allow feelings which oppose God's purposes and so influence your decisions.

Your will is submitted to His purposes as revealed in His Word. You want to see His Word expressed in your life.

God's Spirit cannot influence your thinking, your feelings and your will unless they are surrendered to Him. Only then will you make the right choices and give the correct directions to your body.

If there is not this submission of soul and body to the Spirit, God's order for your life is disrupted (as in the right-hand diagram). This does not infer that you are not a Christian, or that God has removed His Spirit from you. It simply means that you cannot function in the way God intends without this submission to His Spirit.

The Holy Spirit can only be victorious in your life, if you are prepared to be submissive to Him. You will never be victorious in your own strength, but only through submission to the Lord. Faith cannot operate properly without this submission.

This is not a submission to men, but to the Lord Himself and to the integrity of His words of truth.

Jesus walked in constant victory because He lived in perfect faith. This faith was expressed in a life lived in total submission to His Father's will. 'For I have come down from heaven not to do my will but to do the will of him who sent me' (John 6:38).

You will only live a life of faith and be victorious if you follow Jesus. He will lead you along a way of submission to God's will, and obedience to His Word. Only in this way can

your spirit, soul and body be kept under the Lordship of Jesus and the influence of His Holy Spirit.

Those who attempt to live by faith, without such submission, are likely to be disappointed – no matter how many times they claim the promises of God.

Your key to a victorious life:
  SUBMIT YOUR SOUL (YOUR MIND, EMOTIONS AND WILL) TO THE HOLY SPIRIT.

5

Victory through God's Word

The way to victory:
**A life of faith is based on obedience to God's Word. To
live according to His Word is to live in victory.**

Your victory scripture:
**The words I have spoken to you are spirit and they are
life. (John 6:63)**

JESUS IS THE WORD

Jesus is the Word of God. By this Word He created. This
Word became a man and lived among us. So when Jesus
speaks, the Father speaks through His Son, revealing
eternal truth to us. Jesus' words are spirit, life and truth:

Man does not live on bread alone, but on every word that
comes from the mouth of God. (Matt. 4:4)

If you are to live by faith you will not base your decisions on
your own intellect or rational thought, nor on your senses,
but on what God says in His Word. **His words will be a
constant source of life for you and the foundation upon
which you structure your life.**

ROCK AND SAND

Jesus told the parable of the man who built his house on

rock and another who built on sand. The one who built on rock heard God's words and put them into practice. The other heard God but did not do what He said.

The obedient one experienced victory when the storm came. He was able to withstand all the pressures that came against him.

The one who had built on sand had heard what God said, but had not obeyed. He suffered the loss of his house in the storm.

If you are to be a man or woman of faith, you will need to apply God's Word to your life. There is no point in possessing a Bible, reading it and even saying that you believe what is written there, if you are not prepared to put the Word into action. **The one who lives the Word will be victorious.**

Faith is not knowing a series of promises which you claim for yourself. These promises are part of the covenant God has made with His children. He will certainly keep His side of the agreement and will bless you abundantly.

He expects you to live your side of the agreement: to live according to His Word and by the power of His Spirit. This can only be done by faith.

The man of faith realises that the whole revelation of God's Word is for him. He cannot pick and choose what he fancies. There are words to obey and promises to believe. Both belong together.

God intends you to be able to withstand whatever storms batter you, whatever difficulties confront you. **Faith and obedience form the way of victory: hearing God, believing what He says and doing it.**

LIVE THE WORD

The words of Jesus are the answer to every need. It is through His words that believers are set free:

If you hold to my teaching, you are really my disciples. Then you will know the truth, and the truth will set you free. (John 8:31–32)

Many Christians try to find liberty and freedom from their needs and problems in other ways, through techniques in ministry or prayer. It is only the truth of Jesus' words and what He has accomplished, that will actually liberate people.

Jesus says that the Holy Spirit will guide us into all the truth. 'He will not speak on his own; he will speak only what he hears, and he will tell you what is yet to come. He will bring glory to me by taking from what is mine and making it known to you' (John 16:13–14). The Holy Spirit 'will teach you all things and will remind you of everything I have said to you' (John 14:26).

Even God's Spirit does not act in independence. His purpose is to reveal Jesus' words to us so they become revelation in our hearts. Only then can faith be created within us. Only then can we be motivated to obey Him. Then we are able to act upon His words. When we do so, we experience peace. Failure to live God's Word leads to conflict. We then have no confidence before God. When we pray we doubt what the outcome will be. And such doubt prevents both faith and victory.

FAITH AND REASON

There will be many times when you will want to contradict His words with your reason. There will be other occasions when your feelings seem utterly opposed to what God says. At such times you will have to choose whether you will trust your feelings, or believe the truth.

This is one of the most important aspects of a life of faith. The temptation to believe the natural reason rather than the supernatural power of God, will always be with you. Reason limits the Lord in your life; faith releases His activity in your experience.

It is easier to believe reason than revelation.
It is easier to believe feelings than the Word.
It is easier to listen to your doubts than to the Lord.

Easier – but not right.

This is the point of struggle for many Christians. It is so much more reasonable to believe what you can see, touch or feel. **But faith is believing what you do not see.** Are you going to adopt the easy way, or live by faith?

For a whole generation the children of Israel wandered around the wilderness because, when Moses sent the spies ahead into the Promised Land, ten of the twelve believed what they saw rather than the promises God had given them. **They listened to their fears instead of to their faith.**

Only Joshua and Caleb listened to the Lord, believing His words. To Joshua was given the privilege of leading the people into their inheritance. But those who listened to their fears perished in the wilderness. For them the promises and their own ambitions remained unfulfilled.

God is not opposed to reason; He is beyond reason. His thoughts and ways are much higher than your thoughts and ways. **Do not limit the Lord by your reason.**

If God says one thing and you say another, someone has to be wrong! Whenever you contradict the Lord you can be sure He is right. He will not change His Word to accommodate your reason or feelings. **It is your ideas and attitudes which will need to change and be brought into line with His truth.**

Many do not walk in victory and experience triumph in their Christian lives because they choose to believe themselves; to believe what they think or fear, rather than to agree with God's revelation of truth and the promises He gives in His Word. You have to make the decision whether you believe what God says or whether you trust your own wisdom instead.

For the man or woman of faith, there can be no

compromise on this point. You cannot mix a little of the Word with your own wisdom and expect to see great things from God. Your mind will need to be submitted to His Spirit. And He will reveal the truth to you.

Hear the truth.
Believe the truth.
Obey the truth.

The wise man built on rock. If you are wise you will listen carefully to the Lord and put His words into practice. If on the other hand you choose to be foolish, you may hear what He says but trust in your own 'wisdom' instead. Then you will build your house on sand and it will not be able to withstand the storms of life. Are you going to be wise or foolish?

Your key to a victorious life:
  PUT GOD'S WORD INTO PRACTICE.

6

The Victory of Your King

The way to victory:
   If Jesus is your King, He will reign in your life, then you will have confidence before God and be assured of the victory He alone can give.

Your victory scripture:
   Not everyone who says to me, 'Lord, Lord,' will enter the kingdom of heaven, but only he who does the will of my Father who is in heaven. (Matt. 7:21)

YOUR LORD AND KING

If Jesus is your Lord and King your life is to be submitted to His authority; you want Him to rule and reign over you.

This means He is your boss. He is number one in your life. You yield the control of your life to Him, and nothing is allowed to be more important than Him. Nor do people, no matter how much you love them, have any higher place in your priorities or any greater claims upon you than Jesus.

For Him to effect His reign in you, your soul needs to be in submission to His Spirit; your mind, emotions and will submitted to Him. The Spirit directs you to His Word. **To live under the authority of Jesus as His disciple, is to live according to His Word.**

God's promises are linked to obedience and faith. The Christian who seeks to obey Jesus' words but does not believe His promises, will not live in the revelation of God's abundant grace and generosity. The one who believes the promises but does not obey the Word will not be able to appropriate the riches of the inheritance which he claims.

If you are tempted to disobey, the Holy Spirit within you will warn you. If you do not heed His warnings you will find it exceedingly difficult to walk in faith and victory.

FAITH AND OBEDIENCE

Faith within you is inspired by hearing God's words in your heart. The Holy Spirit takes the words of scripture and speaks them to you, so you know you have heard directly from God.

The Holy Spirit will not convict a believer of sin and promise blessing at the same moment. What the Lord does, both in scripture and in the Christian's experience, is to give promise of blessing if there is repentance first.

All these blessings will come upon you and accompany you if you obey the Lord your God. (Deut. 28:2)

To recognise Jesus as your Lord is to respect His authority over you. When your soul and body are submitted to the influence of His Spirit you will be mightily blessed, and will have confidence before God when you pray. You will be able to believe the wonderful promises Jesus gives you.

This is not to be a begrudging submission coming from a rebellious heart, but a willing response to His love. It is love answering love. **In His love God gives; in your love you submit willingly to His authority and obey**. After fifty years of seeing how Jesus' promises worked in practice, John wrote:

Dear friends, if our hearts do not condemn us, we have confidence before God and receive from him anything we ask, because we obey his commands and do what pleases him. (1 John 3:21–22)

Allowing Jesus to be Lord in the daily circumstances of your life gives you confidence before Him. You want to obey Him and do what pleases Him. In response, He wants to bless you and grant the desires of your heart. 'Delight yourself in the Lord and he will give you the desires of your heart' (Ps. 37:4).

Those living a victorious life walk in obedience to Jesus. This is true fellowship. He is the Victor. He is the Answer to every need. And you can live in close harmony and fellowship with Him.

Not only will you be blessed as a result, but others will be blessed because of you. When your life is submitted to Jesus, His Spirit flows out of your life as rivers of living water. And others are blessed with God's love and power because of you.

DISOBEDIENCE BRINGS CONFLICT

If self is raised above Jesus, in effect He is dethroned in your life. He is not allowed to be Lord and King in practice. Several things can cause this: self-concern, fear, worry, anxiety, selfishness, pride, greed, and so on. When you give way to these fleshly things the natural soul life, or 'self', opposes the Spirit and the Word.

This is not necessarily the Christian's desire or intention, but what effectively happens.

Conflict comes from not accepting what God says. The Spirit is leading in one direction, self in another (see figure).

You have confidence in your relationship with Jesus when you are at peace with Him. If there is a conflict of wills, you cannot know that peace, until you are ready to submit to Him. So Jesus says:

> If anyone would come after me, he must deny himself and take up his cross and follow me. For whoever wants to save his life will lose it, but whoever loses his life for me will find it. (Matt. 16:24–25)

WRONG	RIGHT

SOUL – Fear
    Worry
    Anxiety
    Negative feelings
    Selfish motives
    Wrong attitudes
    Weak will
	YOUR SPIRIT INFORMED
	BY THE HOLY SPIRIT

CRUSHED SPIRIT	SOUL – Faith in Word,
	    not reason
	    Listening to Holy
	    Spirit not feelings
	    Determined to obey

Cannot function properly	
the Lord is grieved	

BODY – Expresses fear,
    man-pleasing,
    selfishness
	BODY – Expresses faith,
	    obedience,
	    love

'The measure you give is the measure you receive' is a principle of God's Kingdom. You give your life to Him, He gives His life to you! You give yourself in loving obedience to Him, and He gives the abundance of His riches to you.

This inheritance is yours by faith, and appropriated through obedience. Does this mean you can only receive the Lord's blessing when you have achieved a certain degree of obedience? Not exactly, for **everything you receive from Him is a gift, the result of His grace and mercy.**

However, Jesus expects obedience to what He speaks into your life at any given time. As you grow in spiritual maturity it seems He expects more of you. But the blessings that accompany a growth in obedience also increase. He expects much of those to whom He gives much. **You can be confident in faith when you know you are seeking to fulfil God's will in your life. When you are submitted to Him, His**

Spirit inspires faith within you to believe His promises of victory.

As you submit your life to the sovereignty of Jesus, recognising His rule and reign over you, so you will discover you can then rule and reign over your circumstances in His name. As you acknowledge His authority over you, so you are able to exercise authority yourself.

THE CRUCIAL DECISION

You have to make the crucial decision: Is Jesus going to be on the throne of your life, or do you still want to be in control? He will never force Himself upon you, nor make you do His will. In His Word He shows you His purpose; your obedience is to come from your love for Him. 'If anyone loves me, he will obey my teaching,' Jesus said (John 14:23). **Your love is a response to His love for you. And in His love He wants to provide for you!**

Your key to a victorious life:
    WALK IN OBEDIENCE TO JESUS.

7

Victory in the Mind

The way to victory:
Fill your mind with the positive truth of God's Word and you will be able to refuse, resist and reject all negative input, and will experience victory in your thought life.

Your victory scripture:
Be transformed by the renewing of your mind. Then you will be able to test and approve what God's will is – his good, pleasing and perfect will. (Rom. 12:2)

God wants to influence your thinking by declaring His Word to your heart by the Holy Spirit.

At the same time your mind is battered by three negative influences:

the world
your own flesh
and the devil.

The world around you is full of negative attitudes, ideas and beliefs totally alien to the Christian faith. You have to counter these, so that you are not influenced by them.

Your negative attitudes oppose faith, whether negative attitudes towards problems or people.

When people react negatively towards problems they expose their unbelief:

they worry about the problem
they fear the outcome
they resent the situation
they submit to the need
they accept the sickness.

When reacting negatively to people:

they refuse to forgive them
they judge and criticise them
they resent them
they are jealous of them
they may accuse and condemn them.

The negative situation has not caused these reactions. The difficult problem or person exposes what is already there within the Christian. To the same situation:

A negative Christian will react negatively
A positive Christian will act positively.

The negativity is an absence of faith in that particular situation.
The positive attitude is a demonstration of faith in Jesus.

THE WORLD

Every Christian has to learn how to counter the negative influences in the world around him by refusing to accept them into his thinking. He resists living with the world's values by submitting to those of Jesus. He refuses to think as wordly people do, becoming despairing or despondent. He refuses to be caught up in the desire to outdo his neighbour in material possessions. He refuses to be seduced by the world's dubious business practices and its love of position and esteem.

The best answer to the negative is the positive. It is easier to resist the negative if your life is offered positively to God. If this is the case the use of your time, money and abilities will be firmly under the Lordship of Jesus.

THE FLESH

You have to learn how to counter the negatives within yourself. Although at new birth your thinking changed about many aspects of your personal life and relationships, yet you are not yet perfect in your thinking, just as you are not yet perfect in behaviour. You have the mind of Christ both in the written word of scripture and by the inspiration of the Holy Spirit; but you can still choose to believe your own thinking. This is often negative, because of the negative patterns of thought that have existed in your life over many years.

These may be negatives about yourself, about the kind of person you are and what you can or cannot do. If you consider yourself a failure you will inevitably think negatively in particular situations. If you do, you will not be able to walk in positive faith until your thinking is renewed.

Because you desire to live by faith, **resist all thoughts which accuse you of being unacceptable, unloved, rejected or a failure.**

You are accepted in Christ Jesus.
You are loved by God. He has lavished His love upon you by making you His child and by filling you with the Holy Spirit.
You are not rejected, for there is no condemnation for those who belong to Jesus.
You are not a failure, even though sometimes you fail. Everybody fails at times, but you are not to think you are doomed to persistent failure. You are learning to live by faith with all God's resources at your disposal.

Resist your fleshly desires, not allowing your mind to dwell on proud or selfish thoughts. Resist lustful fantasies, temptations to indulge greed and any unwillingness to forgive. **As soon as you are conscious of such thoughts reject them immediately in the name of Jesus.**

The positive is the best answer to the negative; light dispels darkness. Set your mind on the positive truth and praise God for His victory within you.

THE DEVIL

The enemy tries to bombard the mind of every Christian. But the shield of faith God has given you is able to quench all the fiery darts of the evil one. He wants to undermine your faith in God's Word and encourage you to centre your thoughts on yourself instead. If he can persuade you to believe your own thinking, you will act in your own strength and not in God's supernatural promises.

The devil wants you to act independently of God. This is the way he attacked Jesus in the wilderness. He suggested that He should turn stones into bread to satisfy His hunger. But His Father had not told Him to do this. To obey Satan would be to act independently of His Father's will and direction. Any such action is sinful. If Jesus had yielded to such temptation He would have become imperfect and could not have been our Saviour. Jesus always refused to act independently of His Father.

The devil will try to entice you by encouraging worldliness and stirring up your flesh life. He does not announce his presence, but likes to work subtly. Often his attack is a single negative or enticing thought. But if accepted by the Christian, Satan will follow the first negative with another and then another.

Refuse to accept the first negative thought every time the enemy attacks.

NO CONFUSION

Some express concern because they are not sure whether particular thoughts are from God, the enemy or 'self'. Here the scriptures are your yardstick. **You can safely reject anything that does not conform to the teaching of the New Testament, no matter how reasonable or beautiful the thought may appear to be.**

A good example of this is the statement that everybody will go to heaven when they die. Many worldly people believe this, but it is also a fleshly temptation for the Christian to think in such a way, especially in relation to people he knows and loves. The devil encourages such thinking because it is not true; it conflicts directly with what Jesus and the whole New Testament revelation tells us. Jesus says:

> Whoever believes in him (God's Son) is not condemned, but whoever does not believe stands condemned already because he has not believed in the name of God's one and only Son. (John 3:18)

He says this immediately after making it clear that He did not come to condemn but to save. In His love God the Father has provided us with a Saviour. **But to reject the Saviour is to reject the salvation He offers.** And Jesus clearly states that those who are not with Him are against Him. There is no neutral ground, no fence to sit on and no compromise with the truth.

Faith is undermined by bitter and resentful attitudes towards others, especially those who have caused hurt. This is why Jesus said, 'And when you stand praying, if you hold anything against anyone, forgive him, so that your Father in heaven may forgive you your sins' (Mark 11:25).

If you do not forgive others God will not forgive you. And if you are not forgiven you cannot have confidence before the Holy God, even though He is your Father.

So the enemy will try to persuade you that you are justified in your resentful attitude. You were in the right. It is for the other one to apologise. You ought to feel sorry for yourself for being treated in such a way.

You can recognise easily that such attitudes conflict directly with Jesus' teaching to forgive. So do not listen to anything which conflicts with His will.

FILL THE MIND

The best method of defence is attack. **If the mind is filled with the positive truth of God's Word it will not play host to the negative influences of which we have spoken.** Knowledge of the Bible, and the New Testament in particular, will enable you to discern whether something is right or wrong. The Holy Spirit also helps in this, even when you are ignorant of what the scriptures teach about a particular matter.

There will be times when you sense something is not right even though you may not know why. **Listen carefully to the intuitive warnings of the Holy Spirit.** He will guide you into all truth; He will take what belongs to Jesus and declare it to you.

Remember, God's thoughts are higher than your thoughts. He takes into account the spiritual dimension in every situation. He is supernatural; His power is greater than the natural.

Jesus taught His disciples to think spiritually, to take account of the supernatural resources available to them. An obvious example of this is the miracle of the feeding of the five thousand. When told to feed the crowd, the disciples looked at the situation with the natural eyes of reason and thought the task impossible.

But Jesus knew what He would do to meet the people's need, because He looked with spiritual eyes. He took the supernatural power of God into account. He thought with faith attitudes.

It is not that God wants you to be a non-rational being. He has created you with the ability to reason. **He wants you to expand your thinking, not reduce it. He wants you to think in supernatural, not natural terms, to take into account what God can do by His Spirit when you trust Him.**

Jesus' first disciples did not find it easy to make the necessary adjustments in their thinking; neither will you always find it easy. Making such adjustments is essential to a life of faith, fighting the temptation to limit God by your natural thinking. Your natural thinking will defeat you. **Your supernatural thinking will point you to victory.**

In many situations you will have to decide whether you are going to believe the revelation of God's Word, or your own ideas:

> Are you going to accept what the Lord says, or listen to the negative doubting attitudes of your own mind?
> Are you going to listen to God or men?
> Are you going to believe the truth, or the lying deceptions of the enemy?

As a man or woman of faith you are going to believe God; not yourself, or the world, or the devil – but Jesus!

Your key to a victorious life:
RESIST THE NEGATIVE THOUGHTS WHICH OPPOSE FAITH; FILL YOUR MIND WITH THE POSITIVE TRUTHS OF GOD'S WORD.[1]

---

[1] See Colin Urquhart, *In Christ Jesus* (Hodder, 1981), for a more detailed explanation of your inheritance in Christ.

8

Victory in the Emotions

The way to victory:
   The Lord's love is not dependent on feelings. He wants
   you to live in the power of His Spirit rather than to be
   controlled by your emotions.

Your victory scripture:
   There is no fear in love. But perfect love drives out fear.
   (1 John 4:18)

It is possible to exalt the mind above the Spirit, living by
your own rational ideas instead of through revelation of the
truth in God's Word. Likewise you can listen to your own
feelings instead of the Lord's voice.

Everybody is emotional because everybody has emotions. God has created us with the ability to feel.

A person may be free in his emotions, free to express
love and joy. A fearful person will appear to be frozen
emotionally. He feels as deeply as anyone else but because
of his fear tries to hide his emotional response to people
and events.

The Lord wants you to have a healthy mind, filled with
His thoughts. Similarly **God wants you to be emotionally
healthy.** Just as your mind must not rule your spirit, so
you must not allow your feelings to dominate or rule
you.

NOT FROZEN

The perfect love of Jesus casts out all fear. No statement in scripture is repeated more often than the simple command, 'Fear not.' Fear demonstrates a lack of faith. If your trust is in the Lord, there is no need to fear.

To fear God is to be in awe of Him, not emotionally frightened of Him.

God's love for you is spiritual, not emotional. Your love for Him comes from your spiritual birth, not an emotional response to Him.

However, your love for God cannot be complete unless it touches your emotions. His Spirit is to flow through your soul. Therefore His love is to be expressed in the way you think with your mind and feel with your emotions. **God's love for you is not born of emotion, yet it is to touch the emotions.**

The Christian should not be afraid to feel God's love for him, or to feel love for God. Your relationship with the Lord is neither dependent on nor complete without feelings.

Similarly you can think rationally about God's love for you and your love for Him. But this love is not born of reason; it is born of the Spirit.

If a person has never felt God's love for him, or felt love for God, something is deficient in his relationship with the Lord. Many a 'frozen' person has begun to thaw out emotionally once he or she has received the Holy Spirit. For the first time there is real experience of God's love. There is a release in love, joy, praise and a willingness to witness. What has happened in the human spirit touches the senses, including the emotions.

Emotional insecurity caused by a sense of rejection, failure or inadequacy will make a person fearful of feelings. He fears even God touching those sensitive areas of his life, although His touch is the touch of love which heals and binds up the broken-hearted.

I was an extremely fearful person myself and know what it is to be acutely self-conscious and embarrassed. I would never have chosen a public ministry for myself, especially one in which I had to travel so much, constantly meeting new people.

Feelings of inadequacy dominated my life. So it was wonderful when I experienced Jesus' love for me and knew He had accepted me. But still I needed to be set free to love others and allow them to love me. I did not want people to get too close to me or know too much about me. I must have expended much nervous energy in building and maintaining my defences.

Then the Lord showed me that He loved *me*, not an image of myself that I wanted others to accept. He loved the real me, with all my feelings of inadequacy and failure. He lived in me, not some image of myself. He could work through me despite my weakness.

I needed to forgive those who had contributed to these feelings of inadequacy. I had to ask the Lord to forgive me for living by fear instead of faith. When I truly wanted to be set free, He spoke the word to my heart that set me free and I experienced a fresh release of the Spirit's love in my life.

From that time I have been able to relate far more freely, and have been able not only to love others, but also to allow myself to be loved. Still there are occasions when my natural reaction is to withdraw or hold back. But I have learned that if I listen to my fears I will be paralysed into inactivity. If I listen to words of faith, I can go forward confident of the Lord's enabling:

'Fear not, for I am with you always.'
'I will never leave you, nor forsake you.'
'God has not given you a spirit of fear, but a spirit of power, of love and a sound mind.'

It is certainly not the Lord's purpose that any Christian be rendered inactive through fear. Apart from any other consideration, fear is sin. 'Everything that does not come from faith is sin' (Rom. 14:23). And the Lord always wants to do something about a person's sin!

The Lord wants to heal frozen emotions, but the believer concerned needs to acknowledge:

the sin of his fear
his need of forgiveness
his need of the Spirit
a willingness to be set free.

NOT OVER-EMOTIONAL

A frozen or fearful person is over-emotional, although that is the very thing he or she would deny. Any person whose life is governed by feelings is over-emotional, whether those feelings are negative or positive.

So there are two kinds of over-emotional people:

the frozen, who withdraw behind a shield of silence;
the over-exuberant, whose faith fluctuates with feelings.

Unless the believer submits his emotions to the Spirit they will rule his life. Without this submission he will be dependent on feelings rather than the Lord and His Word.

The one who depends on feelings rather than the Lord, only believes the presence of God if he 'feels' His presence. He believes His love, only if he 'feels' that love. He obeys the Word, if he 'feels' it right to do so. When his feelings are negative because of problems, he quickly panics or even falls into despair. He can easily be made to feel condemned by the enemy's false accusations.

It is impossible to live by faith when so dependent on feelings. **Often the emotional response to a situation will be the opposite to a faith response. The Christian is called to believe the Lord, not his feelings.** Every day of my life I have to walk in victory over emotional feelings. So do you!

When the soul is submitted to the Spirit, the feelings are influenced by the Lord but do not control the believer's decisions. The over-emotional frequently place the soul above the Spirit.

The emotionally insecure are usually spiritually insecure, because they pay so much attention to feelings. Those who are prone to feel rejected may well have problems believing the Lord has accepted them. Those who have felt the need to be self-dependent because they have found it difficult to trust others will find it difficult to trust the Lord. Those who have tried to manipulate others will try to manipulate the Lord.

The Lord does not want your emotions to govern you; He wants you to govern your emotions.

This is possible, even if you have been over-emotional either through fear or an over-dependence on experience. Your emotions are influenced by your thinking. **Right attitudes will lead to right feelings, which in turn will lead to right actions.**

Those with emotional difficulties usually need a renewal in their minds. To seek healing of the emotions is to try to treat the symptom, not the cause.

You can experience victory in your emotions as part of the total victory God wants you to have in your soul.

Your key to a victorious life:
DO NOT ALLOW YOUR FEELINGS TO CONTROL YOU.

9

Victory in the Soul

The way to victory:
  Neither your reason nor your feelings are the truth.
  Jesus is the truth. Believing what He says sets you free
  in your soul – in your mind and emotions.

Your victory scripture:
  If you hold to my teaching, you are really my disciples.
  Then you will know the truth, and the truth will set you
  free. (John 8:31–32)

MIND AND EMOTIONS

The emotions are influenced greatly by the mind. Negative
thinking leads to negative feelings, which in turn lead to
negative actions.

NEGATIVE ATTITUDES
about self, others or situation.

POSITIVE ATTITUDES
about self, others or situation
through faith in the Word.

NEGATIVE FEELINGS
about self, others or situation.
Self-pity and self-concern.

POSITIVE FEELINGS
Confidence through trust in the
Lord. Compassion. Concern
for others. Meets problems
with faith.

NEGATIVE ACTIONS	POSITIVE ACTIONS
governed by fear, unworthiness, low self-esteem, lack of confidence. Criticism, anger or jealousy towards others. Resigned attitude to problems.	Personal boldness in faith. Encourages, forgives, expresses God's love. Attacks problems in Jesus' name.

Ask yourself: Are my feelings in line with God's Word? Are they conditioned by the truth or am I being deceived?

Nobody wants to believe he or she could be deceived. 'The heart is deceitful above all things and beyond cure' (Jer. 17:9). The heart refers to the seat of the emotions and it is here that Christians can be deceived unless they beware. They can be deceived by:

Believing negative feelings to be the truth even though they contradict the Word.

Believing positive feelings based on an emotional response to events. Such responses easily lead to unreality. **An enthusiastic attitude is not necessarily a faith attitude.**

Obviously negative feelings are opposed to the love, joy and peace of God. But religious feelings which may appear to be good are no substitute for the genuine work of the Spirit in the heart and life of the believer. People often mistake soulish experiences, aesthetic experiences of music and drama, for example, as being genuine spiritual experiences. Many non-believers, even those utterly opposed to the Christian faith, have such experiences. They are of the soul, not the spirit. The genuinely spiritual is that which is initiated by God's Spirit. It comes from God, not the soul. Soulish enjoyment and experiences, pleasant though they may be, are no substitute for the true work of God.

It is not going too far to say some forms of worship are aimed directly at the soul, at making people feel good. It is possible to escape reality into a kind of euphoric praise which does not necessarily touch the spirit, but only makes people feel better for a short period of time. Genuine worship in the Spirit leads to an encounter with God which leaves its mark on the worshipper. He knows he has met with the Lord and something has happened in his spirit as a result.

Jesus said, 'God is spirit, and his worshippers must worship in spirit and in truth' (John 4:24). Not in the emotions; in the spirit. What is conceived in the spirit can touch the emotions; but rarely does that which is conceived in the emotions touch the spirit.

THE RIGHT KIND OF MINISTRY

Much ministry that is popular today is aimed at the soul rather than the spirit. Those who receive ministry for their feelings are receiving the wrong kind of ministry. To trifle with people's feelings is only to confirm them in a pattern of behaviour that has already led to failure, defeat or to some bondage of fear and insecurity. To minister to the feelings encourages the person to persist in a life which is based upon feelings.

If you want to build genuine faith into people's lives and help them to experience personal victory, you will need to teach them:

to walk in the Spirit, not in soulish ways:
to depend on God's Word rather than their own feelings.

THE TRUTH SETS THE BELIEVER FREE. **The truth about what Jesus has done for him,** not the facts about all the hurts he has experienced.

What Jesus has made him – he is God's child, a new creation, accepted, forgiven, loved. Negative feelings and dwelling on past experiences tempt the emotional believer to deny the truth.

What Jesus promises him. Ministry directed at the soul concentrates on the self, not the rich inheritance which belongs to every believer.

FREEDOM FROM HURT

Everybody experiences hurt in their lives. Those who we think of as damaged personalities have not necessarily suffered more hurt than others. Often they have not known how to cope with the hurt.

When someone becomes a Christian, he needs to understand he does not have to carry the hurts of his old life into his new life in Christ.

Jesus sets people free from hurt when they forgive those who have caused the hurt. He never used the phrase 'inner healing', but he spoke often of the need to forgive others. A refusal to forgive results in bitterness, resentment and self-pity. These are like spiritual cancer eating away inside the person.

To concentrate on the hurt is to be stuck with it. Jesus met every need on the Cross. He suffered rejection, betrayal, false accusation. He was attacked, beaten and ridiculed.

He took your hurt upon Himself to set you free. All He asks you to do is to forgive those who caused your wounds, even as He forgave those who caused His.

Then you can look to Him for the touch of His healing love. 'It is for freedom that Christ has set us free' (Gal. 5:1)!

Jesus not only wants to set people free; He wants to build them up in the knowledge of His truth, enabling them to walk by faith. Then they will meet future opposition and hurt with forgiveness, not resentment.

If the Christian forgives immediately, he will not be eaten away inside by bitterness or resentment. If he is merciful, he can depend on the Lord's healing mercy.

When you turn to the Lord you expect and receive instant forgiveness, providing you are prepared to forgive others. In the world people want revenge. They like to see those who have caused them hurt suffering in turn. Jesus tells His followers not only to forgive but to love and pray for those who have caused them hurt. What a difference in the two attitudes! Obeying Jesus will prevent future hurts festering and affecting you deeply.

Some very hurt and damaged people may not find it easy to forgive immediately. Forgiveness is not an emotion; it is an act of the will. The Christian decides to forgive. **The right feelings will follow the right decision.**

Receiving God's forgiveness does not depend on feelings, but believing the truth of God's Word: 'If we confess our sins, he is faithful and just and will forgive us our sins and purify us from all unrighteousness' (1 John 1:9). The right feelings will follow the forgiveness, not precede it. When you are forgiven, then you have peace with God. In other words, the emotions respond to what is happening in the spirit.

The same is true with emotional healing. It is not the right feelings that will give the healing, but the activity of God by the Holy Spirit. I would never have received my healing if I had listened to my feelings. Instead I listened to God's words to my heart: 'You are free.'

Later he showed me that if I had not believed what He said I would not have been set free. Accepting that what He said was true led to freedom from emotional bondage.

You do not have to be bound by hurts from the past. You do not have to live in resentment and bitterness any longer. You can choose to forgive all those who have hurt you now. You can come to the Lord with your hurt and be set free. This is God's will and purpose for you. He will minister His truth and His life into your spirit and your whole soul will be liberated by the activity of God's power.

Hear Him speak His words of deliverance to your heart: 'You are free, for the Lord Jesus has set you free.' I have seen countless numbers of people set free through these or similar words.

Do not listen to your feelings; they are not the truth, even though they appear to be the truth at times. Jesus is the truth. What He says is truth. What He has done to meet your need is the real truth. **'And the truth will set you free.'**

THE TRUTH THAT KEEPS YOU FREE

To receive the gift of the Holy Spirit is to receive His power and love for a dynamic life of discipleship. The Christian who is born again and has received the Holy Spirit can rejoice in many truths.

From the very first day of your new birth:

You are forgiven all your past sins.
You are now a child of God.
You are accepted by your heavenly Father.
You belong to God.
You have eternal life.
You have received the gift of God's Kingdom.
You are a new creation.
The old has passed away; the new has come.
You are no longer in bondage to the devil.
God lives in you by the presence of the Holy Spirit.
You have been placed 'in Christ Jesus'.
Every Spiritual blessing in heaven is already yours in Christ.
You have received fullness of life.
You have been given everything you need for life and godliness.
The Lord promises to meet every need of yours because of the glorious riches you have in Christ Jesus.

For the rest of your life you are to live in the truth of the inheritance you received the day you first believed in Jesus. It is these truths which will enable you to live in freedom and faith, not in bondage to your own feelings or fears.

Your key to a victorious life:
BELIEVE WHAT THE WORD TELLS YOU ABOUT YOURSELF – NOT YOUR OWN REASON OR FEELINGS.

10

Victory in the Will

The way to victory:
When you submit your will to God's will you can live in victory. Choosing your own will instead will only lead to frustration, failure and defeat.

Your victory scripture:
Not as I will, but as you will. (Matt. 26:39)

YOUR WILL IS YOUR OWN

God has given you free will. You have the ability to make choices. Your decisions will depend largely on the other aspects of your soul life. **If your mind and emotions are in submission to the Spirit, you will choose to do what God wants.** The alternative is to act independently of the Lord.

An independent person makes independent decisions. His mind is not controlled by God's Word, but by his own natural thinking.

The emotions are conditioned largely by the person's thinking. Negative thinking produces negative feelings and negative decisions. **Positive thinking produces positive feelings and positive decisions.**

There is a certain amount of truth about the power of positive thinking. But we are not concerned here with 'mind over matter'. The Lord wants to see His Spirit ruling over mind and matter. He wishes to influence every aspect of your soul – your mind, emotions and will. Then the activity of God's Spirit can be expressed more fully in your character and behaviour.

If your mind is set on things above, on the words of truth, your emotions will more readily be brought in line with God's purposes, **and you will make the right decisions with your will.**

God will never interfere with your will. He will not force you to obey Him. He reveals His will to you; but in every situation you have the choice to obey or disobey, to please Him or grieve Him.

Neither can anyone else make your decisions for you. When a child you were placed under certain laws at home and school. You were expected to obey. You reacted to your circumstances either willingly or rebelliously. Nobody could determine your response for you.

Now in adult life law is not imposed on you in the same way. You are expected to make responsible decisions. You have to respect the civil laws of the society in which you live; but you can choose to be a law-breaker.

Nobody else can interfere with your ability to choose, and to believe. They can exert pressure and try to influence you. However, you have to choose whether to believe men or God, whether to submit to circumstances or God's Word.

A CRISIS OF LOVE

At times you experience conflict. You know what God is saying to you by His Spirit, either through the scriptures or by direct revelation. But your personal wishes may differ from the Lord's purposes. You know God's will, but do not want to do it. Perhaps you would like to avoid the cost of obedience; or you may hold back because of fear. You may be concerned about the way others will react if you are obedient to the Lord!

Your determination to do God's will is dependent on your

love for the Lord. 'If you love me, you will obey what I command,' said Jesus (John 14:15). The conflict you experience arises out of a conflict of love. Is your love for self greater than your love for the Lord – at that moment, in that situation? If so, you will choose to please self because it is more convenient to do so. **If your love for the Lord is greater than love for self, you will deny yourself, take up your cross and follow Jesus.**

Your love for the Lord is not theory. You may be asked whether you love the Lord more than yourself and answer affirmatively. But the true answer is seen in your choices.

None of us loves the Lord perfectly. Every time we choose self instead of others we show how persistent our love of self can be. And all of us experience the conflict between flesh and spirit.

We learn that making the wrong decisions which deny God's Word and grieve Him never leads to happiness or fulfilment – only to conflict and frustration. Yet in our foolishness we continue to choose self again and again.

The Lord's patience with each of us is truly remarkable. What love was shown by the Prodigal Son's father. He watched the son leave and squander his inheritance through the misuse of his free will, and could only wait for his return. And yet he welcomed his return with open arms embracing him in love and wanting everyone to share in his joy. That boy learned his lesson the hard way and knew he did not deserve his father's patience or forgiveness.

JESUS' EXAMPLE

Life is a series of decisions. Every day you are faced with choices. Many of these are made without much reflection. Some choices are automatic because of the kind of person you are or the nature of the relationship you have with the Lord.

The difficult decisions are those which involve a conflict

of interests. It may be easier to please self, but that does not make it right to do so. Jesus experienced conflict in the Garden of Gethsemane. He sweated blood as He faced the decision before Him, 'My Father, if it is possible, may this cup be taken from me. Yet not as I will, but as you will' (Matt. 26:39).

Humanly He did not want the pain of crucifixion or to suffer separation from the Father, which would be the inevitable consequence of taking our sins upon Himself. But His soul was submitted to His Father at all times. It is His Father's will that matters, not His own. His decisions must not conflict with His Father's purposes. You see in Jesus the act of perfect submission: 'Yet not what I will, but what you will' (Mark 14:36).

Jesus lived in constant submission to His Father and that was the secret of His authority. Although He was the Word of God made flesh He spoke no words of His own, only the words His Father gave Him to speak. He could do nothing by Himself, but did only what He saw the Father doing. All believers need to emulate this example of submission to the Father's will and authority, a submission that comes from love for Him.

FAITH AND AUTHORITY

Jesus saw a close relationship between faith and authority. He commended the Roman centurion for his faith because he trusted in the authority that Jesus displayed. **The man of faith will be a man of authority.**

You are only able to exercise authority if you know how to submit to authority. **The more a Christian recognises and submits to God's authority, the greater the authority he will be able to manifest in his own life and ministry.** And the man of faith needs to exercise authority if he is to be victorious – authority over the enemy, and the mountains or problems which confront him, over his own flesh.

There is a chain reaction which begins with love and which God wants to see operating in your life:

You love the Lord.
Because you love Him, you are willing to submit to His authority and do His will.
This obedience gives you confidence before God.
This confidence is expressed in the authority you manifest as a believer.
This authority is an essential element in your ability to live by faith.
This faith results in victory.

So there is a direct link between your love for the Lord and the victory you experience. That victory is dependent on your expressing your love for the Lord by willingly submitting to His authority over you.

THE RIGHT DECISIONS

You make the right decisions with your will because of your love for the Lord. Submit your mind to the mind of Christ and do not allow your natural emotions to rule and govern your life, particularly in the important decisions you have to make. Do not be surprised when you experience a conflict of interests; that is only to be expected. **By His grace you will make the right choices if your desire is to please Him.**

Should you make wrong decisions choosing to please self instead of the Lord, you will not be condemned. Through His grace and mercy He is willing to forgive as soon as you repent.

This is not an excuse to treat God's will lightly. Before you were a Christian sin had dire consequences in your life as it separated you from the Lord. Sin is no less important now. It may not have the eternal consequences it had before your salvation; but it deeply grieves God and prevents His Spirit from flowing through you in the way He desires.

Jesus waged war on sin. Every believer is to do likewise, first in his own life, then in the world around him. **It matters to God that you please Him by obeying His will.** But still He will not force you to do so.

You grieve Jesus when you consciously or deliberately sin against Him, choosing self rather than the cross of self-denial. Jesus warned that the way would be narrow and difficult. It is so tempting to choose the broad and easy way, especially once you are secure in your salvation.

If your heart is set on pleasing Jesus, you will obey Him. Nothing matters more to you than doing His will.

He will use the disobedient times to show you the self-love which persists within you. But even when you stumble temporarily, He still works within you to bring you back to obedience.

The way of peace is
the way of love, which is
the way of obedience, which is
the way of submission, which is
the way of authority, which is
the way of faith, which is
the way of victory, which is
the way of Jesus.

Your key to a victorious life:
WILLINGLY SUBMIT YOURSELF TO THE AUTHORITY OF JESUS.

11

Victory in the Body

The way to victory:
Victory in the use of your body is a reflection of the victory in your spirit and soul. Your body does not need to rule you; you can rule your body.

Your victory scripture:
Live by the Spirit, and you will not gratify the desires of the sinful nature. (Gal. 5:16)

YOUR BODY IS A TEMPLE

Your body houses your soul and spirit. When you received the gift of God's Holy Spirit your body became a temple of the Holy Spirit. Now God lives in you; His holy presence is within you.

Your body is not only to contain God's life; it is to express that life. The light of Jesus is to shine through your behaviour, attitudes and relationships, in what you say and how you say it. Even your face and general appearance can radiate the joy and peace of God within you.

The human body reflects what is happening in the soul. This was true about Jesus in His humanity as it is true for you. God's Spirit worked perfectly through His soul and body. Because your soul is not perfectly submitted to the Father's authority, His life is expressed only imperfectly in you.

Paul's testimony was clear:

I have been crucified with Christ and I no longer live, but Christ lives in me. **The life I live in the body, I live by faith in the Son of God,** who loved me and gave himself for me. (Gal. 2:20)

The life He lives in the body is a life of faith. So two important truths have to be put together.

1 **The life of God's Spirit will only be expressed through your body if there is the right submission to His will and authority.**
2 **This is only possible if you live by faith.**

To God your body is precious because it is a temple of the Holy Spirit. It is not to be misused or abused.

Satan tempts people to gratify their physical desires in lust and greed because he wants to see the temple defiled. He wants Christians to be lazy so their bodies are not put to proper use.

Whatever happens in the mind and emotions governs the will and this in turn directs the body. In the diagram overleaf the diagram on the right indicates that the sinful use of the body points to a spiritual problem. If the soul is submitted to the Spirit, the believer will not be ruled by his bodily appetites but will deny the cravings of his body in order to glorify God. Without this submission he will be ruled by his desires and will grieve the Lord.

This is not only true in the sexual area of life. The body can express many other ungodly attitudes. Paul mentions hatred, discord, jealousy, fits of rage, selfish ambition, dissensions, factions and envy – to name but a few! But he is quick to point out:

Live by the Spirit, and you will not gratify the desires of the sinful nature. For the sinful nature desires what is contrary to the Spirit, and the Spirit what is contrary to the sinful nature. (Gal. 5:16–17)

RIGHT	**WRONG**
SPIRIT	BODY – craves
MIND	MIND – receives signals from body instead of Spirit
EMOTIONS– –SOUL	EMOTIONS – will only be satisfied if bodily craving satisfied
WILL	WILL – weakened by desire – yields to sin
	– – – – – – – –
BODY	SPIRIT – left out of both decision and action

When you act independently you walk in the flesh, not the Spirit. That is how you lived before you were a Christian. Now you can live dependent on the Lord, trusting to the leading and empowering of His Spirit. Then the fruit of the Spirit is manifested in you: 'Love, joy, peace, patience, kindness, goodness, faithfulness, gentleness and self-control' (Gal. 5:22–23).

The misuse of the body is an ugly thing in God's sight; but its proper use is glorious to Him. **For it is with the body that you do His will, proclaiming the gospel of the Kingdom in word and action.**

> Whatever you do, whether in word or deed, do it all in the name of the Lord Jesus, giving thanks to God the Father through him. (Col. 3:17)

To do everything in the name of Jesus is to do what He would do in your situation. John says, 'Whoever claims to live in him must walk as Jesus did' (1 John 2:6).

Obedience is seen in action. Faith is expressed in action. Once again we see the two together. Paul saw his ministry as calling people 'to the obedience that comes from faith' (Rom. 1:5).

Faith is: **Hearing God's Word**
                Believing what He says
                Acting upon it
Obedience is: **Hearing God's Word**
                Believing what He says
                Acting upon it.

Obedience can only be expressed through faith. And faith is expressed in obedience. What you do in your body will express both faith and obedience, if you submit soul to Spirit. Your love for Jesus will be seen in the way you speak and act. 'Dear children, let us not love with words or tongue but with actions and in truth' (1 John 3:18). If you say you love, perform the actions of love.

RESIST TEMPTATION

Jesus tells us to watch and pray that we may not fall when tempted, for though the spirit is willing, the body is weak. The enemy will try to exploit this weakness through bodily appetites.

Christians do not readily admit to living in a fleshly or soulish manner. They excuse themselves by saying what they did was 'only natural'. They felt it right to 'express themselves'. They remind you that 'nobody is perfect' and suggest that God 'understands their little ways' and makes allowances.

Whenever you are about to sin the Holy Spirit will warn you. If you choose not to heed His warnings and yield to temptation you will lose your peace with God until you have turned back to Him in repentance.

We can praise God for His patience, His grace and His mercy towards us. When we sin He does not cast us off but gently brings us back to the place of obedience, where we rightly belong.

Paul speaks of the enticement of sin that comes to us

through the body; but he also points us to how to live in victory over such temptations.

> For we know that our self was crucified with him so that the body of sin might be done away with, that we should no longer be slaves to sin – because anyone who has died has been freed from sin. (Rom. 6:6–7)

You do not have to be ruled by the body and its appetites any longer. If your soul and body are truly submitted to the Lord, if Jesus is your King and is reigning in your life, you want to please Him. So do not compromise with sin. Paul continues:

> Therefore do not let sin reign in your mortal body so that you obey its evil desires. Do not offer the parts of your body to sin, as instruments of wickedness, but rather offer yourselves to God, as those who have been brought from death to life; and offer the parts of your body to him as instruments of righteousness. (Rom. 6:12–13)

Although you are a new creation, it is still possible to obey evil desires. Your body can be an instrument of either righteousness or wickedness. Before your conversion you pleased yourself and served Satan. Now you can please the Lord and serve Him.

CONSECRATE YOUR BODY

Because you have been brought to life spiritually, you are to offer the parts of your body to the Lord as instruments of righteousness. **Your body is to be consecrated to Him, set apart for His holy purposes.**

There is no limit to the power of God's Spirit within you but His Spirit is housed within the weakness of your mortal flesh. Paul says, 'I put this in human terms because you are weak in your natural selves. Just as you used to offer the parts of your body in slavery to impurity and to ever-increasing wickedness, so now offer them in slavery to righteousness leading to holiness' (Rom. 6:19).

The only way to know victory in the body is to consecrate it to the Lord. To live 'in slavery to righteousness' is only possible if you recognise your body is not your own to do with as you please. **'You are not your own; you were bought at a price. Therefore honour God with your body.'** (1 Cor. 6:19–20) Now you are no longer to bear fruit for death, you are to bear fruit for God!

YOU HAVE DIED

Paul was aware of conflict within himself:

> But I see another law at work in the members of my body, waging war against the law of my mind and making me a prisoner of the law of sin at work within my members. What a wretched man I am! Who will rescue me from this body of death? Thanks be to God – through Jesus Christ our Lord! (Rom. 7:23–25)

There is only one way to overcome the conflict; through Jesus Christ our Lord! 'But if Christ is in you, your body is dead because of sin, yet your spirit is alive because of righteousness. And if the Spirit of him who raised Jesus from the dead is living in you, he who raised Christ from the dead will also give life to your mortal bodies through his Spirit, who lives in you' (Rom. 8:10–11).

To let your life be ruled by your body is spiritual death; to let your life be ruled by the Spirit is life and victory. Each one of us has the choice to make.

Your body is not to rule you; you are to rule your body. Submit your soul to the Spirit and do not be drawn away from God's will by your physical and bodily appetites. To gratify the flesh is only to grieve God and to cause great conflict within yourself.

The way of victory is not to deny the body and its appetites in your own strength, but to **reckon yourself dead to the principle of sin that lives in your body.** This is where faith has to operate.

There have been many occasions when I have fought

battles with myself. I have been aware of desires that oppose God's will for me and have wanted to yield to temptation. The more I have struggled the more intense the battle has become.

Sometimes I have cried out to God to help me, to take the pressure away somehow. I have asked him to change my desires. I have felt such a failure for wanting what displeases Him, even though not always yielding to the temptation.

All these tactics have met with very little success. But time and again the Lord has answered my need by bringing me back to the simple truth: 'You have died.'

Oh, the joy of revelation when the truth comes to your heart afresh! **That's it! I have died!** I do not need to fight the flesh; that only stimulates its activity. I have died. I have been crucified with Christ. It is no longer I who live. Christ lives in me. I have died – and do not have to fight what has died. **Instead of fighting the flesh I can turn away from it and walk in the Spirit.** This is the truth; and the truth works!

You have died and your life is now hidden with Christ in God. That is a statement of truth. Believe it! You do not have to be ruled by your bodily passions. You can obey the leading of God's Holy Spirit, fulfilling His will and His Word.

A NEW BODY

It is not the physical appearance of the body that matters. Irrespective of physical beauty or a lack of it a person can radiate the love, the joy and the peace of Jesus Christ. His beauty can shine through the most ordinary face. The peace and joy of the Lord Jesus flows out of a person's words, attitudes and actions. There is no greater compliment that can be paid to a Christian than for someone to say, 'I can see the Lord Jesus in you.' You can look forward to the time when you will have a new resurrection body that will perfectly reflect the glory of the Lord.

The body that is sown is perishable, it is raised imperishable; it is sown in dishonour, it is raised in glory; it is sown in weakness, it is raised in power; it is sown a natural body, it is raised a spiritual body. If there is a natural body, there is also a spiritual body. (1 Cor. 15:42–44)

Until that time you have to express the life of Jesus in your earthly body. Paul says we are to 'purify ourselves from everything that contaminates body and spirit, perfecting holiness out of reverence for God' (2 Cor. 7:1).

NO NEED TO WORRY

Jesus tells us not to worry about the body's needs:

Therefore I tell you, do not worry about your life, what you will eat or drink; or about your body, what you will wear. Is not life more important than food, and the body more important than clothes? (Matt. 6:25)

If we seek first God's Kingdom and righteousness, He promises He will meet every need. We will not have to worry about the body's material and physical needs.

In other words, if things are in their right order (spirit, soul, body) you can depend on God's faithful provision. Satan seeks to reverse that order, denying God's authority and will. The devil's order is body, soul and forget the Spirit!

You have died.
Your life is now hidden with Christ in God.
You are not your own.
You were bought by Jesus.
He paid the price that you might belong to Him.
Your body belongs to the Father.
He wants to be glorified in the way you see it.

Your key to a victorious life:
CONSECRATE YOUR BODY TO THE LORD.

12
Victory of the Heart

The way to victory:
> If you continually yield your new heart to Jesus, you will express His thoughts, words and actions. A victorious life is a reflection of a victorious heart.

Your victory scripture:
> God has poured out his love into our hearts by the Holy Spirit, whom he has given us. (Rom. 5:5)

THE HEART

The word 'heart' is used in a variety of ways in scripture. At times it is used of the human spirit; the innermost part of the person's being. At other times it refers to the soul, or one particular function of the soul. And there are occasions when it signifies the spirit and soul together.

And yet it is a word used often in scripture and in contemporary Christian terminology. By heart we mean 'man's entire mental and moral activity, both the rational and the emotional elements' (*Vine's Dictionary*). In other words we use this word 'heart' to signify what is going on in us, without trying to analyse too precisely the functions of the 'heart'.

Before you knew Jesus your heart was your own, but when you came to Him you gave your heart to Him. He came to live within your heart, so He can express His life through your life.

*As the heart is to be the governing centre of your whole
being, it is from there, within you, that Jesus wants to
exercise His reign in your life.* The heart makes a person
what he is and governs his actions. It is within the heart that
your true character is formed.

So Jesus said: 'Love the Lord your God with all your
heart and with all your soul and with all your mind' (Matt.
22:37). Every part of your being is to be given to the Lord in
love. For in scripture, to love is to give.

OLD HEART

Before you were born again, your heart was 'corrupt'
because of its self-motivation. Jesus said:

> But the things that come out of the mouth come from the
> heart, and these make a man 'unclean'. For out of the
> heart come evil thoughts, murder, adultery, sexual
> immorality, theft, false testimony, slander. (Matt.
> 15:18–19)

**Whatever exists within the heart will be expressed in a
person's words and deeds.** If the heart is corrupt or unclean,
then he will speak and act in ways unacceptable to God.

Jesus goes beyond the Jewish thought of His day. Under
the Law it was clear what contravened the Lord's commands. However, Jesus teaches that the contemplation of
sin in the heart is as bad as the deed itself.

> You have heard that it was said, 'Do not commit
> adultery.' But I tell you that anyone who looks at a
> woman lustfully has already committed adultery with her
> in his heart. (Matt. 5:27–28)

Jesus was not imposing a new law, the tenets of which were
even more demanding than those of the old covenant. In all
His preaching He aimed at the heart. **If the heart is pure and
consecrated to God, the person's thoughts, attitudes, words**

and actions will be pure and so glorify God. 'Blessed are the
pure in heart, for they will see God' (Matt. 5:8).

Because of the sinful nature of the heart in natural man,
it proved impossible to keep all the commandments. The
Law demonstrated that men would never be able to please
God, or make themselves acceptable to Him, through their
own determined efforts.

Under the promises of the new covenant, the Lord says
He will give His people 'a new heart'.

> I will give you a new heart and put a new spirit in you; I
> will remove from you your heart of stone and give you a
> heart of flesh. And I will put my Spirit in you and move
> you to follow my decrees and be careful to keep my laws.
> (Ezek. 36:26–27)

A new heart will bring new motivation, a new desire to
please the Lord; and the gift of the Holy Spirit will provide
the ability to effect His will.

Under the terms of the new covenant the Lord says: 'I
will put my law in their minds and write it on their hearts. I
will be their God, and they will be my people . . . they will
all know me, from the least of them to the greatest' (Jer.
31:33–34).

THE NEW HEART

**Because you are part of the new covenant, God has given
you a new heart.** 'God has poured out his love into
our hearts by the Holy Spirit, whom he has given us'
(Rom. 5:5).

You are now a son of God with God's Spirit in your heart.
'Because you are sons, God sent the Spirit of his Son
into our hearts, the Spirit who calls out, "*Abba, Father*"'
(Gal. 4:6).

Jesus has 'set his seal of ownership on us, and put his
Spirit in our hearts as a deposit, guaranteeing what is to

come' (2 Cor. 1:22). Paul prays that 'Christ may dwell in your hearts through faith' (Eph. 3:17).

That is the prayer for all who want to live by faith! A prayer for those who were already believers! Without a new heart in which Jesus lives, it is impossible to please God.

Jesus spoke against the religious leaders of His day, because their legalistic observances could not bring about a change of heart, either in their own lives or in those they led. They refused to turn to Jesus to receive the new heart He alone could give them.

> Isaiah was right when he prophesied about you hypocrites; as it is written: 'These people honour me with their lips, but their hearts are far from me.' (Mark 7:6)

A new heart is given to those who surrender the old one to Him. Until that act of surrender, a person can try to serve God through religious zeal – like Saul of Tarsus. He was exceedingly zealous, but blind to the truth. Instead of submitting to Jesus he persecuted those who did so. He must have closed his ears to their testimonies, preferring to hold on to the religious law and traditions of the past. In doing so he genuinely thought he was serving God.

Religious zeal cannot create a new heart. Only God can give that to those who turn to Jesus.

THE OVERFLOW OF THE HEART

Whatever is in a person's heart will be expressed in his words and actions.

> The good man brings good things out of the good stored up in his heart, and the evil man brings evil things out of the evil stored up in his heart. For out of the overflow of his heart his mouth speaks. (Luke 6:45)

A new heart, filled with the life of Jesus, will produce good things. A good heart cannot produce bad fruit, neither can a bad heart produce good fruit.

God has given you a new heart.
Christ lives in your heart by faith.
The overflow of that new heart will produce good fruit.

So do not be drawn back to the past, the old life in which you displeased God. Set your heart on pleasing Him. 'Since, then, you have been raised with Christ, set your hearts on things above' (Col. 3:1).

It is possible for you to set your heart on pleasing self, even though you are a new creation, with a new heart. Or you can daily surrender your heart to the Lord, living to please Him. To 'set' the heart on things above implies a determination to keep looking to the Lord in dependence on Him.

Victory in your heart comes from continual surrender. To turn your heart away from the Lord is to invite failure and defeat, for then you have to depend upon yourself or others; 'See to it, brothers, that none of you has a sinful, unbelieving heart that turns away from the living God' (Heb. 3:12). Paul prays: 'May the Lord direct your hearts into God's love and Christ's perseverance' (2 Thess. 3:5).

I find it important to remind myself that whatever I do or say is a reflection of what is happening in my heart. I can confess sins to the Lord but I will only repeat them, unless I want Him to deal with the heart of the matter. A change of heart will lead to a new attitude, which in turn will affect my behaviour. I need to ask Him to search my heart and show me what is wrong.

Likewise I can only act in faith and experience victory if there is faith in my heart. Many try to put on a performance which they think expresses faith, but without any true revelation of God's Word in their hearts. Then they wonder why things have not happened in the way they wanted.

Jesus went straight for the heart when He taught the people. And when they came to Him for healing, He asked them telling questions which would indicate what they believed in their hearts.

A VICTORIOUS HEART

A victorious heart is one *set* on the Word of God, a heart full of faith. With your new heart you want to be like Jesus and see His life flowing out of you. Jesus wants to reproduce Himself in you. The Holy Spirit makes this possible. You cannot be like Jesus without a heart like His and without expressing victorious faith. For none of His words or actions were superficial; they came from the overflow of His heart, a heart submitted to the will of His Father, a heart which believed His Father could always honour His Words and answer His prayers – a gentle and humble heart.

By contrast the unredeemed heart is aggressive and proud. The evils in the world around us are a demonstration of this. When unredeemed men express what is in their hearts, violence, vice and other atrocities are inevitable.

Those who try to live 'good' lives may manage to contain the more obviously evil traits of their unredeemed nature; but they can never create within themselves the love and presence of Jesus. Nor can they produce His life.

The Holy Spirit is working in you to do just that. He will show you the things which are inconsistent with your new life in Jesus, the pride and selfishness which persist and are evident when your heart is not set on things above.

And He will encourage and create within you the aspects of the personality of Jesus which will please Him. He was never defeated. Because His heart was pure He had confidence and in every situation could exercise the authority His Father had given Him. He was victorious because He had a victorious heart, a clean heart, full of faith – yet He was 'gentle and humble in heart'.

Here is the paradox. **The more humble you are, the more of God's authority you can exercise, just like Jesus.** Even though He is God's Son, He came as a servant, but lived in the fullness of divine power and authority.

Many find it difficult to see that **our confidence before God comes from humbling our hearts before Him and choosing to walk in His ways:**

> Dear friends, if our hearts do not condemn us, we have confidence before God and receive from him anything we ask, because we obey his commands and do what pleases him. (1 John 3:21–22)

Confidence before God will always give you victory, because then you know God hears and answers your prayers. You can pray to Him from your heart, a clean heart, knowing He always answers the prayer of the heart.

God has given you a new heart. But the heart becomes dirty with use, for we live in a dirty world and are not yet perfect in our living of the Jesus life. We can identify with David when he cries out to God: 'Create in me a pure heart, O God, and renew a steadfast spirit within me' (Ps. 51:10).

This He is pleased to do, constantly working within us to refine us. Every branch of the Vine of Jesus is pruned, 'that it will be even more fruitful' (John 15:2).

This is what you want: to be more fruitful for God. This is what glorifies Him, that you bear much fruit, proving yourself to be His disciple. **As a branch of this Vine, with His Spirit within you, you can set your heart on pleasing Him.**

This will involve saying 'No' to those things you perceive to be offensive to His Word and will. When you confess your sin and failure to the Lord, He cleanses you again. He knows you cannot serve Him effectively without regular cleansing of the heart.

The victorious believer is quick to humble himself before the Lord, and is prepared to walk humbly before others in his daily life. He desires earnestly that the Spirit will convict him of any impurity in his heart, any deception or wrong attitude.

His heart is set on the Lord's truth, not on his own ideas or opinions, nor on fulfilling his own desires. He puts his faith in what God says.

Jesus Christ lives in his heart by faith, leading him in His victorious procession. The Christian follows the Man of faith and authority, the Man who lived with a perfect, a gentle and humble heart.

Let Jesus cleanse and refine your heart!

Your key to a victorious life:
SET YOUR HEART ON PLEASING GOD.

13

Victory in Prayer

The way to victory:
>You can experience victory in prayer as you pray in the
Holy Spirit, believing Jesus' promises and persisting in
faith and obedience.

Your victory scripture:
>I tell you the truth, my Father will give you whatever
you ask in my name. (John 16:23)

PRAYER WITH FAITH

Jesus expects His disciples to be victorious in prayer:

>You did not choose me but I chose you and appointed
you to go and bear fruit – fruit that will last. Then the
Father will give you whatever you ask in my name. (John
15:16)

The Lord has chosen you.
He has called you by name, and you are His.
He has appointed you as one of His disciples to be fruitful.

As you fulfil this purpose He gives you this wonderful
promise: 'The Father will give you whatever you ask in my
name.'

This is in line with a series of similar promises Jesus gives.

But we need to take careful note of the context in which He makes these sweeping statements. He promises:

> And I will do whatever you ask in my name, so that the Son may bring glory to the Father. You may ask me for anything in my name, and I will do it. (John 14:13–14)

The word 'And' obviously links this promise to what has been said immediately beforehand: 'I tell you the truth, anyone who has faith in me will do what I have been doing. He will do even greater things than these, because I am going to the Father' (John 14:12).

This must rank as one of the most remarkable of all the statements Jesus made. Anyone (and that includes you!) who has faith in Him will do the same things as He did, and even greater things.

Jesus was about to return to His Father. Then the Holy Spirit would be given to His followers. He would enable them to do the same things as Jesus.

The even greater things are possible because the Spirit has now been given. During the time of Jesus' ministry even He did not pray for people to be baptised in the Spirit, for He makes plain that the Spirit would not be given until He had been glorified. Now He is glorified there are no such limitations. You can pray with others to be filled with the Holy Spirit and God will honour your prayers.

God living in us is even greater than having Him living among us!

We will only do as Jesus did if we act in faith and pray in His name. To pray in Jesus' name is to pray in the way He would pray. There is no set formula of words to use; you pray with the same faith and expectation Jesus would exhibit in your situation.

This is not as impossible as at first it may sound. Because He lives within you by the power of His Spirit, He is present in your situation. **He can show you what to pray and inspire your prayer with faith.**

> But you, dear friends, build yourselves up in your most holy faith and pray in the Holy Spirit. (Jude 20)

Use the gifts of the Holy Spirit, for even when you do not know how to pray, He does. He will not only inspire faith and bring revelation to your heart about the Father's purposes, He will even give you the words which express what is in His heart. The words may be in your own language or in the 'tongue' God gives you by His Spirit. Use that tongue and let the Holy Spirit pray through you.

Faith and prayer belong together in Jesus' thinking. You cannot imagine Him praying without the faith that His Father would answer Him. He not only taught this; He demonstrated it. Standing before Lazarus' tomb He prayed, 'Father, I thank you that you have heard me. I knew that you always hear me' (John 11: 41–42).

Jesus promises He will do whatever we ask in His name when we operate by faith, expecting to do the things He did and even greater things.

This is His word to 'anyone who has faith'. Do you see this as God's purpose for you? As you move out in faith so you will see the Lord honouring your prayer.

WHATEVER YOU WISH

Jesus also said:

> If you remain in me and my words remain in you, ask whatever you wish, and it will be given you. (John 15:7)

This seems an even more sweeping statement: 'Ask whatever you *wish*, and it will be given you.' But there is a condition – 'If you remain in me and my words remain in you.'

When you became a believer God took hold of your life

and placed you 'in Christ'. **You have fullness of life in Him. God blesses you with every spiritual blessing in Him. He will meet your every need in Him. Your life is now hidden with Christ in God.**

Jesus tells you to continue to live in Him. The verb in Greek has a continuous meaning. **Go on living where God has put you – in Christ. Do not live as if separated from Him. Do not walk in your own independent ways; live in Jesus.**

And let His words continue to live in you. Have faith in God and what He says, rather than in the problem or need. Let your life be an example of one who is not only hearing, but putting the Word into practice, with your heart set on doing His will.

Jesus is safe in saying you can then ask anything you wish, and it will be done for you. If you are abiding in Him and His words are living in you, you will not want what is alien to His purposes.

Personal blessing is certainly included in this promise. Jesus is saying: **if you give your life to me in this way, you can be confident I will give you whatever you want.** 'The measure you give is the measure you receive.' He promised:

> I tell you the truth, my Father will give you whatever you ask in my name. (John 16:23)

THE FATHER AND THE SON

Some people are confused as to whether to address their prayers to the Father or Jesus, and whether it is the Father or Jesus who will respond. In these prayer promises Jesus says you can ask the Father or Him, and either will answer. So do not fret over this detail. 'I and the Father are one,' said Jesus (John 10:30). Often you will find yourself praying one moment to the Father and then to Jesus. The formula of words does not matter, but what you believe in your heart.

Whether we pray to the Father or Son, we ask in the name of Jesus. This is the name above every name, the name of the victorious and glorified One. Are you getting the picture? **If you live in His name, you can truly pray in His name** and 'my Father will give whatever you ask in my name'.

Jesus gives these great prayer promises to those who:

**Know they are chosen and appointed to bear lasting fruit.
Live in Christ.
Have His words living in them.
Are living by faith, doing the same things as Jesus and greater things through the Holy Spirit.
Pray in the name of Jesus, with His expectations.**

Victory in prayer comes from a life of faith and obedience.

AGREEING TOGETHER

Again, I tell you that if two of you on earth agree about anything you ask for, it will be done for you by my Father in heaven. (Matt. 18:19)

Jesus does not mean we are to agree to a formula of words when we pray. We are to agree in faith. There is to be a heart agreement.

It requires only two who live in Jesus, and have His words living in them, to agree in prayer. If they agree, both will have the same expectations as to what the Lord will do in response to their prayer. Both will have the same witness of the Spirit in their hearts.

It is possible for someone to pray a prayer and others to respond with the 'Amen', but there is no indication as to what people actually believe. Is there an agreement of faith? Are their lives in agreement with the Word?

Jesus gives this particular promise when talking of

believers' authority to bind and loose, exercising authority over other spiritual powers which can influence lives. We have seen how the exercise of authority is a consequence of submission to Jesus.

He promises that where two or three are gathered in His name He is with them. Clearly He is present to hear and respond to the agreement of faith between His followers. If we pray in His name, then He will agree with the prayer, and it is done.

It may seem that more and more conditions are being made if we are to see those amazing prayer promises fulfilled. We must remember that the fruit of answered prayer is produced in a life of faith and obedience.

This does not mean that only those who have reached a certain standard of discipleship can expect answers to their prayers. EVERY ANSWER IS AN ACT OF GOD'S GRACE AND MERCY. Even the newest Christian can experience mighty answers in prayer. He is fresh but expectant in his faith, and his new heart prompts obedience to the Lord.

Both faith and obedience are essentially simple and are possible for any Christian at any time.

Faith believes God to answer.
Obedience does what God says.

Any Christian can do either at any time.

However, disobedience saps the Christian's confidence. Instead of expecting the Lord to answer, the disobedient are prone to think of reasons why the Lord would be justified in not answering their prayers.

Jesus encourages us in a life of faith and obedience, promising that such a life produces much fruit for the Father's glory and the reward of answered prayer.

Many have lived selfish lives and have been disappointed in prayer and then wondered why. Many have lived disobedient, unbelieving lives and have then complained bitterly because God has not done what they asked. They point to such promises and say they are untrue, or unrealistic, or not for today. But Jesus' message is clear:

If you believe, you will receive whatever you ask for in prayer. (Matt. 21:22)

You could not ask for a more simple, straightforward statement.

FAITH AND AUTHORITY

Faith is the chief element in prayer. And those who live by faith speak not only to the Lord, but to the problem also.

I tell you the truth, if you have faith and do not doubt, not only can you do what was done to the fig-tree, but also you can say to this mountain, 'Go, throw yourself into the sea,' and it will be done. If you believe, you will receive whatever you ask for in prayer. (Matt. 21:21–22)

The exercise of faith involves authority. The man of authority will not only speak to the Father, he will address the situation in the name of Jesus. This is how Jesus operated in faith, authority and prayer; He addressed the need:

'Be opened.'
'Your sins are forgiven.'
'Get up and walk.'
'Peace, be still.'
'Lazarus, come forth.'

To give only a few examples!

You can speak to your problems and needs and see them moved. You can have victory 'if you have faith and do not doubt'.

What if such faith does not exist? Humbly submit

yourself to Jesus, confess your unbelief and ask Him to forgive you. Then ask Him to speak a word of faith into your heart, a word relevant to your situation.

Faith comes from hearing God.

When I teach about these prayer promises, the unbelief which persists in the heart of many Christians is readily exposed. Sometimes I am verbally attacked by those who suggest I should not make such outrageous statements. But the promises do not come from me; they were given by Jesus. Like everybody else I find them both challenging and faith-building.

I know that when I do not see the answers to prayer that are needed the fault does not lie with God. He has not withdrawn His promises, neither has He broken His Word.

Frequently I have to ask myself what I truly believe He will do in answer to my prayer. I ask:

'What do I believe God will certainly do in answer to this prayer?'
'Do I believe I have received the answer, or am I only hoping something will happen?'
'Am I only saying the right words, or do I believe in my heart that He has done it?'

The Lord honours our honesty, but He hates hypocrisy. If I know faith is lacking, I have to ask Jesus to forgive me and then pray the Holy Spirit will speak a word of faith to my heart. Only faith the size of a mustard seed is needed – the faith of God, which He gives.

THE PRAYER OF FAITH

When teaching the disciples how to pray with faith (Mark 11:22–25), Jesus makes four points:

1 **Have faith in God** – not the problem, not yourself, not your fear nor in others – in GOD.

2 **Speak to the mountain of need** – but do not doubt in your heart; believe that what you say will happen. It is the faith of the heart that is victorious, not the form of words.

3 **'Whatever you ask for in prayer believe that you have received it, and it will be yours.'** You receive by faith immediately, when you pray, even though there may not be anything to show at once for such confidence. You receive the answer in your spirit, and know it is only a matter of time before you see the outworking of it.

4 **Forgive any who have wronged you** or God will not forgive you. And nothing hinders the receiving of answers more than unforgiven sin.

FAITH PERSISTS

Ask and it will be given to you; seek and you will find; knock and the door will be opened to you. For everyone who asks receives; he who seeks finds; and to him who knocks, the door will be opened. (Matt. 7:7–8)

Again there is a continuous meaning to the verbs 'ask', 'seek' and 'knock'. This shows us there needs to be a persistence in prayer. We continue to ask, seek, find, believing the promise, 'everyone who asks receives'.

Do not look at your past experience or at the experiences of others. Consider the Word. Listen to Jesus. Believe His promises. He will not reduce the words and promises to the level of your experience. He wants to raise your experience to the level of His Word.

Faith persists and does not give up because the answer is not immediately visible. 'Believe that you have received it, and it will be yours.' If Jesus says it will be, it will be! Believe Him!

Jesus told the parable of the persistent widow (Luke 18:1–8) 'to show them that they should always pray and not give up.'

If you believe, you will receive whatever you ask in prayer. Jesus says so!

This is victorious prayer. Remember it is as possible for the newest Christian as for the mature believer. Any disciple, young or old, can choose to live by faith and in obedience.

FAITH is hearing God.
believing what He says and acting upon it.
OBEDIENCE is hearing God,
believing what He says and acting upon it.

Your Key to a victorious life:
VICTORIOUS PRAYER COMES FROM A LIFE OF FAITH AND OBEDIENCE.[1]

---

[1] For further reading on the subject of prayer see Colin Urquhart, *Anything you Ask* (Hodder, 1978) and *Listen and Live* (Hodder, 1987).

14

Victory over the Devil

The way to victory:
Jesus has already won the victory over the devil and all his angels. He has given you authority over the enemy. You can share in His victory.

Your victory scriptures:
The reason the Son of God appeared was to destroy the devil's work. (1 John 3:8)
I have given you authority . . . to overcome all the power of the enemy; nothing will harm you. (Luke 10:19)

RESCUED

Jesus' victory is complete. The spiritual powers of darkness have been overcome by the Light of the World.

The devil is described as the god of this age, who blinds the minds of unbelievers. He is 'the prince of this world' (John 14:30). This does not imply he has any power, authority or status above that of Jesus. Satan can rule only where he is allowed to rule. Because the world is opposed to God's purposes, Satan appears to hold sway. His influence is seen in many political and social areas of life, for example. But all have sinned and, like the devil, have fallen short of God's glory. So every person is in spiritual darkness until he or she comes to personal faith in Jesus.

At that point the new believer is rescued from the devil's clutches by the Lord:

For he has rescued us from the dominion of darkness and brought us into the kingdom of the Son he loves. (Col. 1:13)

Satan's power is transitory. Jesus is both Lord and King eternally. He has already overcome Satan. The time will come when all the enemy's power will be taken from him, and there will be a new heaven and a new earth.

DELEGATED AUTHORITY

Meanwhile those who exercise authority in the name of Jesus discover they have power over the devil and all his minions. Those who belong to the Kingdom of God have authority over the powers which belong to the dominion of darkness. Jesus told His disciples:

I have given you authority to trample on snakes and scorpions and **to overcome all the power of the enemy; nothing will harm you.** (Luke 10:19)

'Snakes and scorpions' refer to the evil powers which acknowledge Satan. **Jesus gives authority to disciples to overcome *all* the power of the devil. The man of faith does not need to fear defeat from him or any of his forces. Faith in Jesus is more powerful, for His is the name above *every* name.**

Jesus confirmed that He had given such authority to His followers after saying, 'I saw Satan fall like lightning from heaven' (Luke 10:18).

Satan was originally the archangel Lucifer, who led worship in heaven. All that God made was good, including Lucifer. Worship is a response of love to the Lord, and the angels were created as spiritual beings able to love. Lucifer abused this love. Instead of leading others to worship the Lord, he determined that others should worship him.

This one act of rebellion led to his immediate expulsion from heaven, together with one third of the angels who followed him in his rebellion. Jesus witnessed the event.

Satan was given leave to go to and fro over the earth. Now, through temptation, he is used to test men's hearts to see whether they truly remain steadfast to the Lord, or turn away from God in rebellion – like the devil himself.

He even had leave to tempt Jesus in the wilderness at the outset of His ministry. But he could find no way of making Jesus rebel against His Father's will and authority.

LIGHT AND DARKNESS

In him was life, and that life was the light of men. The light shines in the darkness, but the darkness has not overcome it. (John 1:4–5 mgn.)

There is no way that the darkness could overcome the Light. When you shine a torch into a dark room, the darkness has to give way to the shaft of light. The darkness can do nothing to repel the light.

The tragedy is that so many, having naturally rebellious hearts, have followed Satan in rejecting the Light of Jesus. They have refused to repent and turn to Him. So Jesus says:

This is the verdict: Light has come into the world, but men loved darkness instead of light because their deeds were evil. Everyone who does evil hates the light, and will not come into the light for fear that his deeds will be exposed. (John 3:19–20)

Repentance and faith in Jesus deliver you from spiritual darkness. 'Put your trust in the light while you have it, so that you may become sons of light' (John 12:36).

Those who have received the Light of God's truth in

Jesus are to walk in the light. They are to live in light, not darkness.

> I am the light of the world. Whoever follows me will never walk in darkness, but will have the light of life. (John 8:12) I have come into the world as a light, so that no-one who believes in me should stay in darkness. (John 12:46)

Because you live in the light of Jesus, you do not need to fear the darkness. You are no longer separated from Jesus. You live in Him and He lives in you. You live in the Light and the Light lives in you.

You have become light to the world. Light can shine from your life into the darkness. What belongs to the light is positive, while the darkness is full of negatives. God's Kingdom is positive; the dominion of darkness is negative.

You are a child of God's positive Kingdom.
You can reign over the negative.
You are a child of light.
You do not need to fear the darkness.
You can overcome evil in the name of Jesus.
You have authority over the devil and his works.

EXERCISE YOUR AUTHORITY

You need to exercise authority over the devil. There is little point in having such authority if you do not use it!

The devil cannot touch those who are walking in light. Sin and disobedience make Christians vulnerable. While they walk in the light they have no fellowship with the devil and are able to resist him.

Isaiah describes the Way of Holiness:

> The unclean will not journey on it . . . wicked fools will not go about on it. No lion will be there, nor will any ferocious beast get up on it; they will not be found there. But only the redeemed will walk there. (Isa. 35:8–9)

The devil is described as a roaring lion who prowls around looking for someone to devour (1 Pet. 5:8). But no lion can get on to the Way of Holiness. Neither can wild beasts, the demonic forces.

It is as if these animals are on either side of this Way of Holiness. While you walk along the Way of Holiness, living in the light, they cannot touch you. Should you stray from the way, you make yourself vulnerable to their influence.

THE THIEF

Satan has refused to repent, to submit to the Lordship of Jesus, and has been judged for his rebellion. He refused to put faith in Jesus and is condemned for his sin and disobedience. Sentence has already been passed and he will be cast into the Abyss.

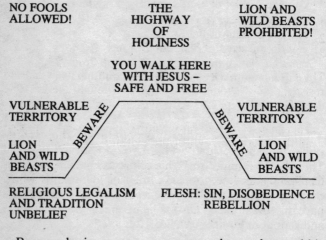

Because he is your enemy, you need to understand his tactics. He is the 'deceiver of the brethren', and can appear as an 'angel of light'. He is a liar, the father of lies and has 'sinned from the beginning'.

Jesus describes Satan as the thief who 'comes only to steal and kill and destroy'. By contrast Jesus came that men 'may have life, and have it to the full' (John 10:10).

The thief comes ONLY to be destructive. This is his purpose – to destroy. He would like to destroy your faith, your health, your relationships, your peace, your life. **But he cannot undo what Jesus has done for you. He cannot take away your eternal inheritance.** But he will try to stop you living in the goodness of that inheritance now.

There is little point in having authority over the enemy if you do not exercise that authority. Why let the thief steal what is yours? **The effect of using your authority is clear: he will flee from you.**

> Submit yourselves, then, to God. Resist the devil, and he will flee from you. (Jas. 4:7)

There is a clear order of events here:

1 **Submit yourself to God;**
2 **Resist the devil;**
3 **He flees from you.**

The Christian who submits to God's authority is able to resist the devil's temptations and his spoiling tactics. The devil flees from the one who lives in obedience and faith.

> Take up the shield of faith, with which you can extinguish all the flaming arrows of the evil one. (Eph. 6:16)

The devil will never relax his efforts to undermine your Christian life. But you have the shield of faith which overcomes all his attacks when put to use. Because you have this shield, use it! Disobedience makes you vulnerable and saps your confidence. So:

> Be self-controlled and alert. Your enemy the devil prowls around like a roaring lion looking for someone to devour. Resist him, standing firm in the faith. (1 Pet. 5:8–9)

Resist the enemy in faith.

Paul says we are not unaware of his schemes (2 Cor. 2:11). He loves to cause division and strife, even among Christians. He appeals to people's pride and encourages unforgiving attitudes towards others. He knows that if you do not forgive others, God will not forgive you, and then you are vulnerable to his devices.

> Do not let the sun go down while you are still angry, and do not give the devil a foothold. (Eph. 4:26–27)

A person is deceived when he believes he is right, but is not. How important to test the things we believe and do against God's Word. If they do not agree with His revelation, have nothing to do with them, no matter how good they may appear to be.

Many have been sucked into false religions and cults through such deceptions. Many Christians have fallen into sinful relationships through deception; what appeared to be good at first can end in grievous sin. Why believe Satan or any demon, when he is the father of lies.

SATAN'S MOUTHPIECE

Even a disciple can be used as Satan's mouthpiece, as Peter discovered to his cost. One moment he was used to speak mighty revelation from the Father, stating that Jesus is the Christ, the Son of God. Soon afterwards he hears these stinging words from Jesus: 'Get behind me, Satan! You are a stumbling block to me, you do not have in mind the things of God, but the things of men' (Matt. 16:23).

Why should Jesus speak such words to him? Because Peter had dared to contradict Him when He spoke of His coming rejection and crucifixion. This did not fit in with Peter's views of Messiahship, or his desires for the Master he loved. But who was he (or any man) to argue with God's Son, or to disagree with His words?

Christians today can be used by the enemy to speak against the truth, if they listen to their own ideas or traditions which are a contradiction to the revealed truth of the scripture. That is like the clay telling the Potter that he doesn't know his business.

This is real deception. Anything which opposes the truth is a lie. And we know the identity of the father of lies! Jesus told those who opposed His teaching that their father was the devil.

John says: 'He who does what is sinful is of the devil, because the devil has been sinning from the beginning.' But immediately points out:

> The reason the Son of God appeared was to destroy the devil's work. (1 John 3:8)

He has done just that.

Jesus has destroyed deception by revealing the truth.

Jesus is the true Light of the world. He does not appear as a false angel of light.

Jesus is righteous. He does not lie like Satan.

Jesus came to give abundant life, not to steal love, faith, health and happiness.

Jesus gives eternal life. He does not want any to be condemned.

Jesus overcame the devil on the cross, that you might overcome him in your life.

Jesus came to destroy the devil's work to give you victory over him.

WHOSE CHILD ARE YOU?

The one who is born of God will not continue to sin, says John. And so it is apparent 'who the children of God are and who the children of the devil are' (1 John 3:10). The one who is truly born of God will do what is right and will love his brother. When he sins the Holy Spirit will convict him and lead him back to obedience.

Some of the parables Jesus taught show that God's children and those of the devil grow up together. But when the Day of the Lord comes there is to be a glorious sort out! In the parable of the weeds, for example, 'the weeds are the sons of the evil one, and the enemy who sows them is the devil' (Matt. 13:38–39). They will be sentenced to 'the fiery furnace'.

By contrast, 'the righteous will shine like the sun in the kingdom of their Father' (v. 43).

You are not a child of the evil one; **you are God's child. His plan for you is that you will shine like the sun in His Kingdom. He wants you to live as a righteous one,** resisting every attempt of the devil to encourage you to live unrighteously.

Above all, the enemy wants to steal the revelation of God's Kingdom from people. He wants to eat the seed spread by the Sower, for he knows that once a Christian has received the revelation of the Kingdom, he is able to exercise the authority of the King over the powers of darkness. **He will not steal this revelation from you. 'Whatever you bind on earth will be bound in heaven, and whatever you loose on earth will be loosed in heaven' (Matt. 18:18).**

God has given you His Kingdom.
You are a child of God.
You do not need to continue to sin.
You do not want to contradict Jesus, or serve the devil in any way.
You do not need to be afraid of him; if you resist him he will flee from you.
He cannot steal your inheritance.
He is no longer your father; God is now your Father.

So do not give any opportunity to the devil. As you follow Jesus, submitting yourself to Him, you can take the shield of

faith and overcome all the devil's attacks on you. As you walk the Way of Holiness, he cannot touch you. As you exercise your Kingdom authority over him, nothing can harm you.

Your key to a victorious life:
   YOU HAVE AUTHORITY OVER THE DEVIL AND ALL HIS WORKS.[1]

---

[1] For further teaching on the victory you have over the enemy, see Colin Urquhart, *The Positive Kingdom* (Hodder, 1985).

15

Victory in Spiritual Warfare

The way to victory:
Exercise the authority over the enemy Jesus gives you
as a child of His Kingdom.

Your victory scripture:
Do not rejoice that the spirits submit to you, but rejoice
that your names are written in heaven. (Luke 10:20)

DEMONS

Some Christians have over-emphasised the significance of
demons, holding them responsible for every negative thing
in a person's life, believer or non-believer. Others have
underestimated their importance or have denied they have
any influence at all.

Jesus believed in the existence of both the devil and
demons. To explain away the gospel references to the
demonic by saying that Jesus was using the thought forms
of His day, is nothing short of blasphemous. This is to
accuse Jesus of deception. He constantly put right other
contemporary misconceptions. It is unthinkable that He
would speak to the devil and demons if they did not exist!

We see the right balance in Jesus' ministry. There were
occasions when He commanded demons to come out of
sick people. At other times He spoke a simple word of
healing. He exercised discernment, knowing when the

problem was a specifically demonic one. Jesus freed a demonically possessed and very violent man. 'He had often been chained hand and foot, but he tore the chains apart and broke the irons on his feet. No-one was strong enough to subdue him' (Mark 5:4).

Jesus spoke to the demonic presence with authority: 'Come out of this man, you evil spirit!' The evil spirits were given leave to enter a herd of pigs, which 'rushed down the steep bank into the lake and were drowned' (Mark 5:13).

This demonstrated the destructive nature of these demonic powers, but also the authority of Jesus over them. And this was by no means an isolated event.

> When evening came, many who were demon-possessed were brought to him, and he drove out the spirits with a word and healed all the sick (Matt. 8:16).

These demonic powers can cause physical impediments: 'Then they brought him a demon-possessed man who was blind and mute, and Jesus healed him, so that he could both talk and see' (Matt. 12:22). He knew when the demonic powers were the direct cause of the sickness and therefore had to be confronted. It seems that Jesus did not pray to the Father on such occasions; He addressed the demons.

AUTHORITY OVER DEMONS

Jesus gave His disciples authority over evil spirits and power to heal the sick:

> He called his twelve disciples to him and gave them authority to drive out evil spirits and to heal every disease and sickness. (Matt. 10:1)

This authority was not confined to the twelve. When the seventy-two returned from their mission they were overjoyed, 'Lord, even the demons submit to us in your name' (Luke 10:17).

Of all the things they had seen happen, this impressed them the most. Jesus immediately pointed them to the reason why they had such authority: **'Do not rejoice that the spirits submit to you, but rejoice that your names are written in heaven'** (Luke 10:20).

Because they belonged to the Kingdom of heaven, they had authority over the spirits which belonged to the dominion of darkness. The real cause of joy is the fact that they belong to the Lord's Kingdom; their names are written in heaven.

This is also true for you. **Your name is written in heaven; you are a child of God's Kingdom. You have the same authority as those first disciples.** If you doubt that, consider what Jesus said next.

> At that time Jesus, full of joy through the Holy Spirit, said, 'I praise you, Father, Lord of heaven and earth, because you have hidden these things from the wise and learned, and revealed them to little children. Yes, Father, for this was your good pleasure'. (Luke 10:21)

Do you consider yourself a little child in spiritual things? You qualify. Do you feel foolish before those with worldly wisdom? You qualify. Do you feel weak in yourself? You qualify. It has been the Father's good pleasure to choose you, to redeem you and invest in you the authority of His Kingdom!

> But God chose the foolish things of the world to shame the wise; God chose the weak things of the world to shame the strong. (1 Cor. 1:27)

You do not need to fear demons if you recognise you have authority over them. You simply need to know how to deal with them so that they do not influence your life in any way. Jesus said:

> How can anyone enter a strong man's house and carry off his possessions unless he first ties up the strong man? Then he can rob his house. (Matt. 12:29)

Jesus has bound the strong man and defeated him. In his name you can do likewise. 'I tell you the truth, whatever you bind on earth will be bound in heaven, and whatever you loose on earth will be loosed in heaven' (Matt. 18:18).

There was a time when I did not believe in the existence of demons. Involvement in the healing ministry changed my thinking. I saw the Lord healing many people, performing mighty miracles. But there were the stubborn cases that did not seem to respond to prayer in the usual way.

'Address the evil.' This was a command the Lord gave me when praying with someone. When I obeyed, the person was set free from a long-standing condition.

That prompted me to look at the gospels with fresh insight and to be open to the Holy Spirit to show me when such prayer was necessary. If Jesus needed to take authority over demonic powers, we will certainly need to do likewise.

DISCERNMENT

You do not have to allow the enemy to harass you. It may seem that one thing after another goes wrong or you seem to come under attack from sickness regularly. As you pray about the situation little seems to happen. When you take authority over the enemy the harassment ceases.

The discerning of spirits is one of the gifts of the Holy Spirit. The use of this gift will enable you to recognise the nature of the opposition, whether it is demonically inspired or not. Do not fear to use this gift. The demonic problems are simple to deal with because of the authority you have as God's child.

This does not imply that demons 'possess' you. They can certainly attack you, but you have power and authority over them.

Every Christian should be alert to the need to rebuke the enemy at times. Remember, the best method of defence is attack. This does not give you a 'deliverance ministry'. I am not speaking about ministering to others, but walking in victory yourself.

You do not need a formula. **You have authority and faith in the name of Jesus. Exercise that authority and use that faith.** Do not anticipate a battle, but complete victory.

There will be times when you need to bind the enemy in prayer; when praying for non-believers to be converted, for example. Remember, the god of this age has blinded their minds. They cannot understand the truth even though you may have tried to persuade them on many occasions. You need to pray for them, but also to pray against the enemy who has blinded them. When he is bound it becomes possible for the person to *hear* the gospel, although he will still need to come to a place of personal response.

There will also be occasions when you will need to bind the spirits of infirmity which can cause sickness.

> Jesus rebuked the demon, and it came out of the boy, and he was healed from that moment. (Matt. 17:18)

You can do this in prayer, using the name of Jesus. Remind yourself and the enemy that you are under the protection of the blood, and that nothing can harm you.

I am not advocating that you undertake personal ministry with those who you think may have a demonic problem. That is best left to those with pastoral responsibility and experience.

It also needs to be said that many think their problem is demonic when it is not. It is convenient to blame the enemy for sin and disobedience which are the responsibility of the individual Christian. If the father of lies can persuade a believer he is 'possessed' or in bondage to the devil, he has been allowed a victory which should never have been given to him. He is a liar.

Refuse to accept any of his lying accusations. Live in personal victory, not allowing the enemy to bring you into any false bondage, condemnation or confusion. Remember, neither the lion nor any wild beasts can walk in the Way of Holiness.

Keep walking along that Way!

Your key to a victorious life:
YOU HAVE AUTHORITY OVER DEMONS BECAUSE YOUR NAME IS WRITTEN IN HEAVEN.

16

Victory over Opposition

The way to victory:
   Rejoice in the face of opposition. Maintain an attitude of love, mercy and forgiveness towards those who oppose you.

Your victory scripture:
   Love your enemies, do good to those who hate you, bless those who curse you, pray for those who ill-treat you. (Luke 6:27–28)

FAITH OVERCOMES THE WORLD

Jesus does not promise His followers an easy life. 'In this world you will have trouble,' He says (John 16:33). However the verse continues: 'But take heart! I have overcome the world.'
   Because you live in Jesus, you can live in His victory. John says:

   This is the victory that has overcome the world, even our faith. Who is it that overcomes the world? Only he who believes that Jesus is the Son of God. (1 John 5:4–5)

To whom are these words addressed? **'Everyone born of God.' That includes** *you.*
   Because you are a Christian, born again of the Holy Spirit, **you have overcome the world. You can be victorious no matter what the world does to you.**

John talks about the exercise of such faith within the context of obedience. God's commands are not burdensome to those who love Him. The one who obeys has overcome the world, which is opposed to faith and God's Word because of the rebellion that pervades fallen mankind.

YOU ARE BLESSED

The believer can expect opposition because those of the world live by an entirely different set of values to his own. In fact, the Christian is blessed when he meets with opposition, even of an unjust kind:

> Blessed are you when people insult you, persecute you and falsely say all kinds of evil against you because of me. Rejoice and be glad, because great is your reward in heaven. (Matt. 5:11–12)

> Blessed are you when men hate you, when they exclude you and insult you and reject your name as evil, because of the Son of Man. Rejoice in that day and leap for joy, because great is your reward in heaven. (Luke 6:22–23)

When confronted with such opposition it takes a man of faith to react by leaping for joy! Paul was such a man, which was why he could sit in prison and write to the Philippians telling them to rejoice in the Lord always. He teaches that we are to give thanks in all circumstances, because this is the will of God for us in Christ Jesus.

To respond to opposition with such joy and thanksgiving is evidence of faith. The believer keeps his eyes not on the opposition, but on the Lord. It does not matter what he has to suffer for the sake of the Kingdom. He cannot expect understanding, or even justice, from a fallen world. But he knows Jesus has perfect understanding of every predicament in which he can find himself. The Lord will always treat him with justice, love and mercy.

LOVE YOUR ENEMIES

So Jesus tells us to go further still in our attitudes towards opposition:

> But love your enemies, do good to them, and lend to them without expecting to get anything back. Then your reward will be great, and you will be sons of the Most High, because he is kind to the ungrateful and wicked. Be merciful, just as your Father is merciful. (Luke 6: 35–36)

In all these scriptures Jesus emphasises that the believer's reward will be great in heaven. Why worry about the way the world treats you now? No one can steal your heavenly inheritance, and when in heaven, you will receive no further opposition from the world.

Jesus tells us to love our enemies and be merciful towards them.

> **Love your enemies, do good to those who hate you, bless those who curse you, pray for those who ill-treat you.** (Luke 6:27–28)

Love, do good, bless and pray! What a contrast to the way people usually react to opposition and hate. The natural reaction is to complain, return the hate, feeling bitter and resentful, demanding revenge and punishment for those who have caused the problems. All such reactions belong to the world, not to God's Kingdom, and are destructive of faith if they are found in a Christian. He will have to repent of such reactions, no matter how justified they may seem to be.

What a contrast; and what a witness it can be to the world when a Christian acts in love and forgiveness. I think of a Christian couple being interviewed on television following the murder of their daughter. They expressed only sorrow for the one who had perpetrated such a crime, stated clearly that they had forgiven him and even wanted to visit him in prison to share Jesus with the murderer.

What a contrast with those of the world who in similar circumstances scream out for vengeance and retribution.

Opposition can hurt, especially when untrue things are said about you. Jesus knows we cannot be shielded from hurt; it is part of the inevitable cost of living the gospel in a fallen world. But He shows us how to react to such opposition.

When you rejoice in the face of opposition, any hurt is short-lived. Your heart goes out to those who have caused the hurt. You realise that much of the opposition comes from a lack of spiritual understanding.

What really hurts is opposition from other Christians, often through jealousy or prejudice. You know such opposition is ungodly and it is not always easy to maintain a loving, forgiving attitude.

JESUS' EXAMPLE

You only have to look at the example Jesus gave to see how to cope with opposition. He was not passive when issues of truth were at stake, pointing out the hypocrisy of much of the religious legalism of His day. The religious leaders were determined to kill Him, because he was a threat to their traditions, their positions of esteem and their system of religious conformity. They hated Him and were plotting to murder Him long before the crucifixion. But they were unable to have their way before God's appointed time.

When He was arrested it was out of jealousy, not justice. The charges were false and the witnesses did not agree. But whenever falsely accused, Jesus refused to reply to the charges.

Here is an important principle for every Christian. **You do not have to justify yourself, for God ensures the truth is vindicated,** even if this takes time. In Jesus' case it took three days. The resurrection was total vindication; but even so His opponents did not want to believe.

The only time Jesus answered Pilate was when He was directly challenged as to who He was. To remain silent then would have been to hide the truth. But He did not have to answer false accusation.

What a difficult lesson this is for many Christians to learn! This is the true meaning of turning the other cheek.

It is your faith which HAS OVERCOME **the world. The power of the Kingdom is greater than that of the world.** The former is spiritual, the latter is temporal. The first is supernatural, the second natural. The Kingdom is eternal, the world finite. So keep your eyes on Jesus and the victory He has already won!

You do not have to behave like others around you. You do not have to conform to worldly values and patterns of life. You do not have to allow yourself to be sucked into the world's negativity: bitterness, resentment, hatred, malice, greed, envy, and so on.

The victory of faith in Jesus overcomes all the worldly attitudes with which you can be confronted.

When you are insulted, rejoice.

When you are persecuted, you are blessed.

When you are falsely accused, remain silent; the Lord will vindicate you.

When you are rejected for your faith in Jesus, remember your reward is great in heaven.

When you are faced with continual opposition, be thankful that Jesus is with you.

When you are opposed by enemies of the gospel, love them.

When you are treated ungratefully, continue to be kind and merciful like Jesus.

When you are hated, do good to those who hate you.

When you are cursed, bless those who curse you.

When you are ill-treated, pray for those who cause the hurt.

When your faith is challenged, speak boldly in the name of Jesus.

You can rejoice in the face of all opposition, knowing you are blessed and that the Lord will reward you for remaining true to Him. You can answer opposition with the love and forgiveness Jesus demonstrated.

This is the gospel of Jesus. He died to make it possible for you to react in such ways. He took all your negativity to the Cross that you might be filled with the positive virtue of His love.

Your key to a victorious life:
YOUR FAITH OVERCOMES THE WORLD AND ALL THE WAYS YOU CAN BE OPPOSED.

17

Victory Attitudes

The way to victory:
As you believe what God says about you in His Word,
you will be able to live in faith and victory. You are
more than a conqueror, able to reign in life.

Your victory scripture:
No, in all these things we are more than conquerors
through him who loved us. (Rom. 8:37)

MORE THAN A CONQUEROR

Do you approach problems negatively or positively, with
unbelief or faith? **You are more than a conqueror.** This is
not a statement to make you feel better when you feel low;
it is the truth about you because you live in Christ and can
never be separated from His love. **God wants you to have a**
faith attitude as a way of life. You cannot turn faith on and
off like a light switch.

'Who shall separate us from the love of Christ?' asks
Paul. 'Shall trouble or hardship or persecution or famine or
nakedness or danger or sword?' (Rom. 8:35). He then
proceeds to answer his own questions:

No, in all these things we are more than conquerors
through him who loved us. For I am convinced that
neither death nor life, neither angels nor demons,

neither the present nor the future, nor any powers, neither height nor depth, nor anything else in all creation, will be able to separate us from the love of God that is in Christ Jesus our Lord. (Rom. 8:37–39)

Do you believe this? Do you accept what the scriptures say about you?

I was not brought up with faith attitudes in my early Christian experience. When I was first ordained the Lord told me that He would teach me to believe His words instead of questioning everything He said. My mind and reason had to become submitted to His truth.

Little did I realise the full implications of this at first. Over the years my faith has been enlarged as I have applied one truth after another to my own life.

I would certainly not have thought of myself as being 'more than a conqueror'. But then I did not expect to see mighty miracles or dynamic answers to prayer either. Such things were for a bygone age, or for people of great spiritual stature. They were certainly not for the likes of me.

How wrong can you be! For I came to understand that the truths of scripture are for every Christian, including me. It is true for everyone who is born again that nothing can separate him or her from the love of God revealed in Christ Jesus. Any believer can be 'more than a conqueror' in his daily walk with God – even me!

I began to apply the truths of the Word to myself in very direct and personal ways, realising God was speaking to me about me. From these verses in Romans 8, I learned:

In all things God works for my good, because I love Him and have been called according to His purpose.

God knew me even before I was born.

He predestined me to be conformed to the likeness of His Son.

He called me.

He justified me, making me acceptable in God's sight.

He has glorified me. He already sees me in the ultimate
   victory of His glory.
If God is for me, who can be against me?
He will graciously give me all things.
Jesus is interceding for me at God's right hand.
Nothing can separate me from the love of Christ.
In the face of any difficulty I am more than a conqueror
   through Him who loves me.

I did not always understand the full implications of what I
read. But this was God speaking to me about me! Who was
I to argue with Him? I had to learn to see things as He did,
for He would never deceive me.

**Nothing, absolutely nothing, can separate you from
God's love because your heavenly Father has placed you in
Christ Jesus. This is the basis of your confidence. You are 'in
Christ' no matter what your situation or problem. You are
more than a conqueror through Him who loves you.**

PERSEVERANCE

Jesus has already conquered. You are more than a
conqueror because you can enjoy His victory without
having to fight His battle! Do not resent your problems; see
them as challenges which can lead to the strengthening of
your faith.

Consider it pure joy, my brothers, whenever you face
trials of many kinds, because you know that the testing of
your faith develops perseverance. Perseverance must
finish its work so that you may be mature and complete,
not lacking anything. (Jas. 1:2–4)

Resentment is negative; joy is positive. Just as one who is
persecuted needs to 'leap for joy', so you can rejoice in the
trials of your faith. **Jesus has not abandoned you; He is with
you in the middle of what might appear to you to be mess,
muddle and confusion.**

Your faith will not develop, neither will you grow in spiritual maturity, without having to face trials of many kinds. **Do not expect to be overcome by your difficulties. Anticipate that Jesus will carry you through. Do not become preoccupied with the problem. Do not allow the need to become bigger in your vision than the One who is able to meet that need. And know you will be blessed as you persevere in faith.**

Blessed is the man who perseveres under trial, because when he has stood the test, he will receive the crown of life that God has promised to those who love him. (Jas. 1:12)

Every problem is a challenge to trust Jesus and see how He will lead you through to victory.

NEGATIVE AND POSITIVE

The one who approaches problems without positive faith is doomed to failure. Faith works negatively as well as positively. You anticipate disaster or sickness and it will come upon you. When Job experienced a series of disasters at Satan's hands, he said: 'What I feared has come upon me; what I dreaded has happened to me' (Job 3:25).

Fear is negative faith. This is why the Lord says again and again: 'Fear not.'

The negative person expects the worst and when problems arise accepts them with resignation. He may even believe this to be the right spiritual response, humbly accepting whatever happens as God's will.

This conflicts seriously with Jesus' attitudes. He taught His disciples to speak to the mountains and command them to move. This is going on to the attack, rather than receiving passively whatever happens.

A faith person is a positive person.
He resists the negatives.

He affirms the positive truths of his life in Jesus.
He believes God's promises.
He attacks problems.
He anticipates victory.
He knows nothing can separate him from Jesus' love.

REIGN IN LIFE

Repentance is the answer to the problems you cause yourself. You can learn to react joyfully to persecution, and to exercise authority over the enemy. There are times when you need to confront your circumstances for you perceive clearly that what is happening is not according to God's Word, and is therefore inconsistent with His will.

You have received God's abundant provision of grace and of the gift of righteousness. Therefore you are to reign in life through Jesus (see Rom. 5:17). You are to rule over your circumstances instead of allowing them to control you.

This requires a complete change of attitude for some Christians. They do not realise that God has given them the capacity to possess a faith that can rule. Yet this was God's intention for all men.

> Then God said, 'Let us make man in our image, in our likeness, and let them rule over . . . all the earth.' (Gen. 1:26)

Man's ability to rule was lost when he sinned. But Jesus came with the gift of the Kingdom. Those who have faith in Him and receive His gift have the ability to rule restored to them.

You have received God's Kingdom.
The Kingdom is within you.
You are to reign in life.
YOU ARE NOT THE VICTIM; YOU ARE THE VICTOR.

You will be surprised to discover how readily God rewards your militant faith attitude.

The military analogy does not come easily for some, but is certainly biblical. You are to 'fight the good fight of faith'. And when you fight do not anticipate failure and defeat!

There will be times when you feel indignant with the devil for the sickness, chaos or confusion he has created in people's lives. Come against him in righteous indignation.

It is not only the major problems which test your faith. You will need to be victorious in numerous seemingly trivial matters. **React to every situation with faith, not with fear, despondency or expectation of failure.**

If you do not learn to deal with the foothills, you won't fare very well with the mountains! Jesus wants to train you to have the right faith attitudes in every situation.

You are not to switch faith on and off when it suits you. It is to be a way of life.
You are to live in victory.

Your impulsive natural response to a crisis may be negative; but if you are sensitive to the Word and Spirit, your negative reaction will be immediately obvious to you. Without delay you can ask Jesus to forgive the negative response and begin to affirm the positive answer to the situation. This is something that you have to do. Nobody can do it for you. Faith is not a matter of sitting back and waiting for something to happen.

You have faith; put it into operation. Believe the positive answer to the negative problem.

In your particular situation, what would Jesus do? How would He think? What would His attitude be? Would He passively accept the problem? Would He speak to the mountain? Would He take authority over the enemy? Would He believe His Father to give Him complete victory? How would He pray? What results would He expect from His prayer?

You will be surprised how readily you will be able to answer such questions. And when you are perplexed you can look to the Holy Spirit to show you what Jesus would have said and done.

If you do everything in the name of Jesus, you will emulate His example. When faith is lacking, you can confess your unbelief and ask the Lord to speak a Word of faith to your heart. For there will certainly be occasions when you know what Jesus would have believed and done, but have to recognise a lack of similar faith in your own heart.

Faith involves determination. You are not prepared to accept any answer; only the right answer. And that is the way Jesus answers those who trust Him.

When answers come which only partially resolve a situation, you need to question seriously whether they are given by God, or whether you have responded fully to what He has said. **Do not accept the mediocre when He wants to give you the best.** In Christian things, the good is the enemy of the best.

JESUS IS KING
He is reigning.
You are reigning in Him.

Your key to a victorious life:
MAINTAIN A POSITIVE, FAITH ATTITUDE AT ALL TIMES.

18

Victory through Forgiveness

The way to victory:
  The way of victory is the way of love. The way of love is
  the way of forgiveness – always!

Your victory scripture:
  In everything, do to others what you would have them
  do to you. (Matt. 7:12)

PEOPLE CAN BE PROBLEMS

At times life seems full of problems. Some of these may be
of our own making. We have disobeyed and our sin has
created difficulties we would not have had otherwise.

Other problems arise from the enemy's attacks on us.
These may be times when we yield to temptation he which
places before us. Or we may experience opposition as we
seek to live truthful, righteous and godly lives in an unrighteous world. Sometimes there is no apparent reason for
the difficulties we face. But nearly all our problems involve
people!

Problems are often people and people are often problems.
We live in an imperfect world among imperfect people.
The sins of others can influence our lives, sometimes in
significant and even disastrous ways.

By the same token our sins can have serious repercussions in others' lives especially those who are close to us at
work, in church or at home.

Some say their sins are a private matter between God and themselves. This is not the case, for **sin is a social disease with social consequences.**

Problems arise because we live in a fallen world among fallen people. But even in the Christian community we are dealing with others, who like ourselves, are in the course of being refined and perfected, but have not yet attained that goal. Jesus says:

> My command is this: Love each other as I have loved you. Greater love has no-one than this, that he lay down his life for his friends. You are my friends if you do what I command. (John 15:12–14)

LOVE EXPRESSED IN FORGIVENESS

Love conquers all. This is the Christian message. Jesus' love on the Cross overcame sin, sickness and even death. He sends His disciples into the world with the message of love.

This is not some sentimental kind of cosiness, but the practical way of overcoming the problems people cause, while at the same time reaching out to them in the name of Jesus.

At the heart of love is forgiveness. You could not know God's love for you without experiencing His forgiveness. **You are to extend that forgiveness to others, whoever they may be, regardless of what they have done.** The fellowship Christians enjoy together should be marked by love, forgiveness and acceptance of one another.

The one who refuses to forgive has surrendered to defeat in that particular situation and this can have serious repercussions in his life. The one who forgives experiences spiritual victory and knows he is at peace with God, others and himself.

How often have people prayed, 'Forgive us our sins, as

we forgive those who sin against us', while harbouring grudges or even feelings of hatred towards others. Jesus explained:

> For if you forgive men when they sin against you, your heavenly Father will also forgive you. But if you do not forgive men their sins, your Father will not forgive your sins. (Matt. 6:14–15)

To forgive is to be victorious. To resent is to accept defeat until you are prepared to forgive.

> Do not judge, or you too will be judged. For in the same way as you judge others, you will be judged, and with the measure you use, it will be measured to you. (Matt. 7:1–2)

As a Christian wanting to live by faith, adopt the attitude that you are not going to accept failure and defeat. You want to be victorious in every situation in life. And life is made up of people, and the relationships you have with them. You are going to be victorious by maintaining loving, forgiving, merciful attitudes.

Jesus died to free you from the judgment you deserved. Why put yourself back under judgment by judging others? The way in which you judge them will be the way you are judged. No wonder, then, that Jesus encourages you to 'Be merciful, just as your Father is merciful' (Luke 6:36).

THE GOLDEN RULE

In everything do to others what you would have them do to you (Matt. 7:12).

Do you want to be judged?
Do you want to be criticised?
Do you want to be condemned by others?
Do you want to be hated?
Do you want to be resented?

Of course not. **So do not judge, criticise, condemn, hate or resent others. Every time you resist the temptation to do so, you are victorious.**

Do you want to be forgiven?
Do you want to be accepted?
Do you want to be loved?
Do you want to be encouraged?
Do you want to be blessed?

Of course you do. **Then forgive, accept, love, encourage and bless others. Every time you do so, you are victorious.**

CORRECTING OTHERS

There will be occasions when it is right to correct others. Jesus gives clear direction as to how to do this:

If your brother sins against you, go and show him his fault, just between the two of you. If he listens to you, you have won your brother over. (Matt. 18:15)

That is indeed victory and is far more likely to be gained this way than by openly criticising and speaking against him. Jesus continues:

But if he will not listen, take one or two others along, so that 'every matter may be established by the testimony of two or three witnesses'. If he refuses to listen to them, tell it to the church; and if he refuses to listen even to the church, treat him as you would a pagan or a tax collector. (Matt. 18:16–17)

Jesus wants the man to have plenty of opportunity to repent of his sin before more stringent measures are taken against him. **But notice that the man is judged by the Church, not by the individual.** This leaves no room for personal animosities or vendettas.

The time to go to a brother or sister you believe has sinned, is when you know you can go in love and not judgment, in a spirit of forgiveness not resentment.

BE MERCIFUL

Jesus gives us the parable of the unmerciful servant to reinforce this teaching on mercy and forgiveness. He tells the story in response to Peter's question as to how often he should forgive his brother. He suggests seven times as being appropriate. But Jesus responds: 'I tell you, not seven times, but seventy-seven times' (Matt. 18:22), signifying an infinite number.

A servant owed his master an enormous amount. The servant's master took pity on him, cancelling the debt. But the servant refused to forgive a fellow-servant a petty amount and had the man thrown into prison.

The master was furious when he heard what had happened: 'Shouldn't you have had mercy on your fellow-servant just as I had on you?' he asks (Matt. 18:33). In anger, the master had the servant thrown into prison until he had paid his debt. 'This is how my heavenly Father will treat each of you unless you forgive your brother from your heart,' concludes Jesus (Matt. 18:35).

Jesus is not asking for some token, formal act of forgiveness, but a heart-felt letting go of anger and resentment, treating the brother as if the sin no longer existed.

This parable has serious implications, for it is clear the unmerciful servant had his debts restored, not removed!

God has put His love into your heart by the Holy Spirit. You have the grace to forgive, to know you are at peace with others, that you harbour no bitterness, neither do you hold on to any resentment. Praise God for being free of such negative attitudes.

As the Lord has had mercy on us, so His mercy can be seen

in you day by day, as you maintain an attitude of forgiveness towards anyone who may inadvertently or even deliberately hurt you.

Do not wait for their apologies before you forgive. In your heart forgive immediately the deed is done, so that no root of bitterness can grow in you.

Your key to a victorious life:
    LIVE WITH AN ATTITUDE TOWARDS OTHERS OF LOVE, FORGIVENESS AND MERCY.

19

Victory in Relationships

The way to victory:
   Love is your way of life, giving as well as forgiving.

Your victory scripture:
   Do everything in love. (1 Cor. 16:14)

CALLED TO PRACTICAL LOVE

You are to forgive others. You are also to encourage them
and build them up in love. Paul gives clear, practical
instruction about relationships:

Love must be sincere.
Hate what is evil; cling to what is good.
Be devoted to one another in brotherly love.
Honour one another above yourselves . . .
Share with God's people who are in need.
Practise hospitality.
Bless those who persecute you; bless and do not curse.
Rejoice with those who rejoice; mourn with those who
   mourn.
Live in harmony with one another . . .
Do not repay anyone evil for evil . . .
If it is possible, as far as it depends on you, live at peace
   with everyone.
Do not take revenge . . .
Do not be overcome by evil, but overcome evil with good.
                                                (Rom. 12:9–21)

Many other passages could be quoted with similar instructions.

The best answer to the negative is to be full of the positive. It is far easier to maintain an attitude of mercy and forgiveness towards others when you are full of love yourself.

Love is the fulfilment of the law. You are to love with all your heart, mind, soul and strength. You are to love your neighbour as yourself. And Jesus has given the new command: to love one another as He has loved us.

Let no debt remain outstanding, except the continuing debt to love one another, for he who loves his fellow-man has fulfilled the law. (Rom. 13:8)

When Jesus baptised you in His Holy Spirit, He flooded your heart and life with His love. You now have His resources to enable you to fulfil these commands of love.

If you know you lack such love, ask Jesus to fill you with His Spirit. He promises that everyone who asks receives.

AGAPE – LOVE IN ACTION

God is love. The nature of His love is expressed in giving. Jesus demonstrated this love in action. He showed that love is at the heart of God's purposes. He did not speak often about love; He simply did it!

Paul describes the nature of God's love, the same love He gives to you through the Holy Spirit.

In place of the word love, you can put the word 'Jesus' and know that every statement rings true. It is a humbling exercise to substitute 'I' instead of 'love'. You are immediately conscious of the inadequacy of your love.

This is not a negative exercise. These statements about love describe the life God is forming in you. He wants you to see yourself living in such love. This is the faith picture He wants you to have about yourself. If you anticipate

failure you will certainly fail, but as you realise the Holy
Spirit within you is the Spirit of love, so you will understand
He can express this quality of love through you.

Love is	Jesus is	I am	patient
Love is	Jesus is	I am	kind
Love does not	Jesus does not	I do not	envy
Love does not	Jesus does not	I do not	boast
Love is not	Jesus is not	I am not	proud
Love is not	Jesus is not	I am not	self-seeking
Love is not	Jesus is not	I am not	easily angered
Love	Jesus	I	keep(s) no record of wrongs
Love does not	Jesus does not	I do not	delight in evil
Love	Jesus	I	rejoice(s) with the truth
Love	Jesus	I	always protect(s)
Love	Jesus	I	always trust(s)
Love	Jesus	I	always hope(s)
Love	Jesus	I	persevere(s)
Love	Jesus	I	never fail(s)

(1 Cor. 13:4–8)

This is an exercise I do personally from time to time,
checking my relationships against this description of love,
seeing in what ways my attitudes fall short of God's
purposes. I find it humbling, but rewarding. The Lord
forgives my failure and I can see clearly the areas where I
need to bring my life more fully into line with His will, by
the grace and power of His Holy Spirit.

Faith without love is worth nothing. 'The only thing that
counts is faith expressing itself through love' (Gal. 5:6). Set
your heart on expressing such love in your life.

'Do everything in love', says Paul (1 Cor. 16:14). If you
ask the Holy Spirit to help you, He will enable you to act in
love.

Be imitators of God, therefore, as dearly loved children
and live a life of love, just as Christ loved us and gave

himself up for us as a fragrant offering and sacrifice to God. (Eph. 5:1)

This love is a response to God's love for you. Just as you can see the need to be merciful to others, because of the way the Lord has been merciful to you, see also your need to love others because of the great love He has for you.

This is how we know what love is: Jesus Christ laid down his life for us. And we ought to lay down our lives for our brothers. (1 John 3:16)

This has to be done in practical ways, seeking to meet each other's need, whether of a spiritual or material nature. The one who loves is born of God and knows God, and He wants to see you living in the victory of love. 'If we love one another, God lives in us and his love is made complete in us' (1 John 4:12).

Jesus demonstrated a victorious life through love. It is for us to learn how to meet every situation with love. It is not enough to know this is what we ought to do; we need to do it in practice. It does not honour the Lord if you have faith without love. He wants to see faith in love being expressed in your life.

Every day the Lord puts before you opportunities to reach out to others in love, or to speak words of faith and encouragement to them. Empty platitudes are meaningless. **It is no use telling people you love them unless your words are supported by appropriate action.**

What does it mean to 'be devoted to one another in brotherly love' (Rom. 12:10)? Such a statement cannot be fulfilled if you have a casual attitude towards relationships.

If a brother has a need, you are victorious when you provide for that need. And you will experience a deep sense of satisfaction that God could use you to express His love to another.

To refuse to meet the need when the Spirit is urging you to do so is failure. Such disobedience disappoints the Lord.

He loves you so much. He wants to see you sharing His love with others. You cannot take every burden on yourself and the Lord does not intend you to do so. But God places certain people and needs before you and His Spirit prompts you to take action. 'Share with God's people who are in need' (Rom. 12:13).

FAILURE TO LOVE

Pride and selfishness are the most common causes of failure in love. Some think certain tasks are beneath them, forgetting they are to prove faithful in small things. Jesus came as a Servant, and the greatest in the Kingdom are those who regard themselves as least of all.

Some want recognition, appreciation, applause and praise from others instead of obeying the injunction to 'honour one another above yourselves'!

There are those who will find excuses if an act of love would prove inconvenient or demanding. They are content to leave the costly tasks to others, perhaps claiming this particular job is not their ministry, or they have no specific word about it from God. They will only 'practise hospitality' when it suits them, and will be very careful about who should be the recipients of their hospitality.

Some are happy to rejoice with those who rejoice, but avoid those who mourn. They are content to slap them on the back with what they consider a suitable platitude: 'Cheer up!' 'The Lord loves you.' 'Look to Jesus.' 'Praise the Lord – anyway.'

All truth has to be communicated in love! There are those who are more interested in being right than in expressing love. With such people the truth comes across in a cold, harsh manner – not at all the way Jesus communicated with the people. They seem to speak more in judgment than love, and easily make people feel condemned rather than convicted.

Then they wonder why they are not victorious in

communicating the truth. The fault cannot be in themselves, of course! It must be the hardness of heart and rebellion of the others. More condemnation!

What is the point of telling people there is no condemnation in Christ, when your whole manner and approach only makes people feel condemned?

There are those whose idea of love is to keep themselves to themselves. 'I don't want to bother anyone,' they say. 'My religion is a personal matter between God and myself.'

Perhaps they fear relationships, imagining they will be rejected or considered unacceptable. At the same time they are likely to be inwardly angry that they are not loved and appreciated.

FREE TO LOVE

The way to receive is to give. This is true of love, as of every other aspect of life. It is a spiritual truth of God's Kingdom. Until a person is willing to give himself in relationships, he will always feel a failure.

He will become victorious only when he allows himself to be set free by the truth. In Christ he is loved, accepted, forgiven, appreciated and liberated. In love Jesus sets him free to enable him to love others.

Make every effort to add to your faith goodness; and to goodness, knowledge; and to knowledge, self-control; and to self-control, perseverance; and to perseverance, godliness; and to godliness, brotherly kindness; and to brotherly kindness, love. For if you possess these qualities in increasing measure, they will keep you from being ineffective and unproductive in your knowledge of our Lord Jesus Christ. (2 Pet. 1:5–8)

You are free to love.
God has put His own Spirit of love within you.
He does not want you to think of yourself as a failure in
**   relationships, for love never fails.**

It is not by striving or self-effort that you will grow in love.

Look to the Holy Spirit every day.
Call on Him for help whenever your love seems shaky.
Remember the One who lives within you is patient and kind.
He is ready to work through you.
He will enable you to protect, hope, persevere – and not fail!

Your key to a victorious life:
EXPRESS YOUR LOVE FOR OTHERS IN GIVING TO THEM IN PRACTICAL WAYS.

20

Victory in Giving

The way to victory:
Give generously and joyfully and you will prosper. This is God's will for you.

Your victory scripture:
Give, and it will be given to you. A good measure, pressed down, shaken together and running over, will be poured into your lap. For with the measure you use, it will be measured to you. (Luke 6:38)

A PROSPEROUS PEOPLE

God intends His children to prosper financially and materially. The Old Testament evidence is clear: He promises prosperity when His people are obedient, living in the holiness which is His purpose for them. This contradicts the misconception that equates holiness with poverty.

The Lord will establish you as his holy people, as he promised you on oath, if you keep the commands of the Lord your God and walk in his ways. Then all the peoples on earth will see that you are called by the name of the Lord, and they will fear you. **The Lord will grant you abundant prosperity.** (Deut. 28:9–11)

Israel's 'abundant prosperity' is evidence to other nations that they are the Lord's people, singularly blessed by Him.

However, this prosperity is dependent on their obedience and holiness.

If they became complacent and rebelled in their prosperity (as they did), they were warned they would return to poverty. **Poverty is a curse for the nation's disobedience.** So the alternatives were clear.

> See, I set before you today life and prosperity, death and destruction. (Deut. 30:15)

If His people love the Lord, walk in His ways and keep His commands, they will prosper.

Has God changed? Are not the promises of the new covenant even greater than those of the old? Is not Jesus the 'Yes' and 'Amen' to all of God's promises?

> Walk in all the way that the Lord your God has commanded you, so that you may live and prosper and prolong your days in the land that you will possess. (Deut. 5:33)

If the people obeyed the covenant between God and themselves they would prosper in everything they did.

David was an anointed man with an inspired perception of spiritual truth. The man who fears the Lord, he says, 'will spend his days in prosperity' (Ps. 25:13). **The righteous will flourish** (Ps. 72:7). And he prays:

> Remember me, O Lord, when you show favour to your people, come to my aid when you save them, that I may enjoy **the prosperity of your chosen ones.** (Ps. 106:4–5)

Has the Lord not saved you? Are you not one of His chosen ones? Then He wants you to enjoy prosperity. David says that 'blessings and prosperity will be yours' (Ps. 128:2) if you fear the Lord and walk in His ways.

AN EXPRESSION OF HIS HEART

Several of the Proverbs speak clearly of the Lord's desire to see His people prosper.

> My son, do not forget my teaching, but keep my commands in your heart, for they will prolong your life many years and bring you prosperity. (Prov. 3:1–2)

Once again, prosperity is linked with obedience, this time of the individual, rather than the nation.

The Lord gives prosperity because He is the Lord of prosperity: 'With me are riches and honour, enduring wealth and prosperity' (Prov. 8:18). His purpose is to make us as He is, because we are made in His image. If He prospers, He wants His children to prosper.

'A generous man will prosper' (Prov. 11:25). This is in line with Jesus' teaching that the measure you give is the measure you receive. 'Prosperity is the reward of the righteous' (Prov. 13:21). He has made us righteous in Jesus, that we might live in righteousness and enjoy the rewards of the righteous!

> Whoever gives heed to instruction prospers, and blessed is he who trusts in the Lord. (Prov. 16:20)

> **Faith is hearing the Word,
> believing what God says and
> acting upon it.**

If you do this you will prosper. By contrast, 'A man of perverse heart does not prosper' (Prov. 17:20).

'He who cherishes understanding prospers' (Prov. 19:8)! 'He who pursues righteousness and love finds life, prosperity and honour' (Prov. 21:21)! 'He who trusts in the Lord will prosper' (Prov. 28:25)!

The message is clear. **The man who walks in faith, love**

**and obedience, will prosper. He will prosper in practical,
material ways, as well as prospering spiritually.**

The believer's prosperity comes from the Lord. 'I bring
prosperity and create disaster, I, the Lord, do all these
things' (Isa. 45:7). He does not want to bring disaster on
His people; that is only a last resort when they are deliberately and persistently rebellious. His purposes are good:

'I know the plans I have for you,' declares the Lord,
'plans to prosper you and not to harm you.' (Jer. 29:11)

Although there are times when He needs to punish them,
He promises He will restore prosperity to His people as
soon as they return to His ways.

When the Lord speaks prophetically to His people of
what He will do when the new covenant is established, He
says:

You will be my people, and I will be your God. I will save
you from all your uncleanness. I will call for the corn and
make it plentiful and will not bring famine upon you. I
will increase the fruit of the trees and the crops of the
field. (Ezek. 36:28–30)

This speaks very definitely of a material prosperity. And
this is indeed what we see in the New Testament.

GIVING AND RECEIVING

Jesus teaches you to give, for this is the outworking of love.
But He makes it clear that God will outdo you in giving.
The measure you give will determine how much you are
able to receive from the Lord. This does not imply that you
can buy blessing. The freedom and generosity with which
you give is an indication of what is in your heart.

It is not the amount you give, as Jesus made clear when
the rich were putting their gold into the Temple treasury,
while the poor widow could only give her last two small
coins. This was a far greater offering because it represented

all she had. It demonstrated faith, that she would trust the Lord to provide for her. Paul explains the principle:

> Remember this: Whoever sows sparingly will also reap sparingly, and whoever sows generously will also reap generously. Each man should give what he has decided in his heart to give, not reluctantly or under compulsion, for God loves a cheerful giver. (2 Cor. 9:6–7)

> **Sow generously,**
> **You will reap generously.**
> **Do not give reluctantly.**
> **Give cheerfully.**

How will the Lord respond to generous, cheerful giving? With abundant grace. He gives to the undeserving. We cannot purchase or earn His gifts. All He gives comes by His grace.

> **And God is able to make all grace abound to you, so that in all things at all times, having all that you need, you will abound in every good work.** (v. 8)

This is indeed prosperity:　　in All things,
　　　　　　　　　　　　　at all times,
　　　　　　　　　　　　　having ALL that you need.
Why should God be prepared to give so abundantly?

> **You will be made rich in every way so that you can be generous on every occasion.** (v.11)

Made rich IN EVERY WAY. Then 'you will abound in every good work'; 'you can be generous on every occasion.'
It was while telling about 'this grace of giving' which results in such generosity from God, that Paul said:

> **For you know the grace of our Lord Jesus Christ, that though he was rich, yet for your sakes he became poor, so that you through his poverty might become rich.** (2 Cor. 8:9)

Obviously Jesus has made us rich in *every* way, and that includes financial and material blessing, as the context makes clear. Jesus Himself said:

> And everyone who has left houses or brothers or sisters or father or mother or children or fields for my sake will receive a hundred times as much and will inherit eternal life. (Matt. 19:29)

You cannot outdo the Lord in giving. He calls you to a sacrificial life of yielding yourself completely to Him, obeying His Word and walking in righteousness. He calls you to express your love and faith in giving to Him and to others. But look what He promises in return!

> **Give, and it will be given to you. A good measure, pressed down, shaken together and running over, will be poured into your lap. For with the measure you use, it will be measured to you.** (Luke 6:38)

The principle applies to every area of life including forgiveness, mercy, love, money. The same principle works negatively too. Judge and you will be judged. Refuse to forgive and you will not be forgiven.

The message is simple. **In whatever area of life you honour God, He will honour you. In whatever ways you are generous, He will be far more generous in return.**

If you want to be victorious in the financial department of your life the message is clear:

> **Keep the commands of the Lord your God as one of His holy people.**
> **Walk in His ways and obey His Word.**
> **Give yourself in love to the Lord and others.**
> **Honour the Lord in your resources.**

Do not be deceived: God cannot be mocked. **A man reaps what he sows** (Gal. 6:7).

I would need to write a whole book to give adequate

testimony about how I have seen these principles work in practice. Both in my personal life and in the ministry of which I am a part, I have experienced God's amazing generosity. He has supplied tens, and sometimes hundreds of thousands of pounds in answer to prayer, without any money-raising activities.

But He has impressed on us the need to be faithful in giving, expecting Him to measure back His abundance. There have been times when I have given away thousands of pounds, usually when we have needed even greater sums for ministry projects.

To the reason it seems crazy to give away when you need. But we are living according to the principles of God's Kingdom. And I know the truth of God's Word. We always receive His 'good measure, pressed down, shaken together and running over'. Then we will have more to give away where it is needed.

This is faith in action.

FAITH, OBEDIENCE AND PROSPERITY

So the Bible does not speak of a material prosperity detached from a life of faith, love and obedience, but of a prosperity that will be the outcome of such a life. We are not taught to seek material blessing apart from our life in the Kingdom, but as a witness to others of the goodness of the Lord expressed to those who belong to His Kingdom.

The one who sows to please his sinful nature, from that nature will reap destruction; the one who sows to please the Spirit, from the Spirit will reap eternal life. (Gal. 6:8)

So we are not to become weary in doing good, in loving and in giving. We will reap the harvest at the proper time if we do not give up.

To believe certain promises is not a passport to instant financial riches. To give your life to Jesus, in whatever society, nation or situation you may be, enables Him to give Himself to you in the fullness of life. And you can experience His love and care in abundance, so that you are able to demonstrate His generosity to others, financially and in other ways.

The worst thing you can do when in need is to stop giving. Remain faithful, honouring the Lord and His Word, and He will honour His promises in your life. Like Paul you may experience times of plenty and times of need. God will use both. **In the times of plenty you can bless others. In the times of need you can listen attentively to what God is saying to you.** Nothing encourages us to listen more than need.

The Lord wants you to believe in His grace and generosity.
He wants you to give freely – in every way.
He wants to give to you generously – in every way.

Your key to a victorious life.
WALK IN FAITH, LOVE AND OBEDIENCE AND YOU WILL PROSPER.

21

Victory over Selfishness

The way to victory:
   Never become weary of giving to others.

Your victory scripture:
   A man reaps what he sows. (Gal. 6:7)

LOVE IS GIVING

God is love. The nature of His love is expressed in giving in every area of life. His purpose for us is expressed in love; to love the Lord whole-heartedly, to love our neighbours as ourselves, to love one another as He has loved us.

This purpose can only be expressed in giving: giving to God, to your neighbour, to your fellow Christians. This giving can involve any and every part of your life, making your time, abilities and money available for His use. Above all, making yourself available to Him.

Selfishness is the opposite to giving. It is wanting to receive rather than give; it is holding on to what you have instead of making it available to the Lord and to others.

Do not be deceived: God cannot be mocked. **A man reaps what he sows.** The one who sows to please his sinful nature, from that nature will reap destruction; the one who sows to please the Spirit, from the Spirit will reap eternal life. (Gal. 6:7–8)

'A man reaps what he sows.' This is a spiritual principle, which Jesus applies in several different areas of teaching:

> Blessed are the merciful, for they will be shown mercy. (Matt. 5:7)
>
> For if you forgive men when they sin against you, your heavenly Father will also forgive you. (Matt. 6:14)
>
> So in everything, do to others what you would have them do to you. (Matt. 7:12)
>
> Do not judge, and you will not be judged.
>
> Do not condemn, and you will not be condemned.
>
> Forgive, and you will be forgiven.
>
> Give, and it will be given to you . . .
>
> For with the measure you use, it will be measured to you. (Luke 6:37–38)

You do not want to sow to please your sinful, selfish nature. You want to sow to please the Spirit, to give cheerfully, lovingly, generously, faithfully.

To give in such a way is to experience victory over your naturally selfish instincts. Failure to give is defeat in that particular situation.

The selfish one does not want to give and may refuse to do so. If he does give and gains some advantage, he is likely to be content and not allow himself to be stretched in further giving.

Some years ago I found it necessary to ask the Lord to give me a generous heart, which would reflect something of His own generosity. He answers such prayers when He knows this is what is desired seriously, and is not just a sentiment being expressed because it seems a good thing to pray.

CONTINUAL GIVING

The life of the Christian is one of continual giving, being content to serve in whatever way the Lord asks irrespective of how menial the task may seem. For Jesus makes it clear it is only when you have proved faithful in little things, giving yourself wholeheartedly to the Lord, that you will then be put in charge of greater Kingdom responsibilities. So Paul encourages us:

> **Let us not become weary in doing good, for at the proper time we will reap a harvest if we do not give up. (Gal. 6:9)**

There are times when you give so continuously it is tempting to stop giving. It may be you receive little in return at first. Your giving may be rejected, taken for granted, abused or misused. But the promise is that if you continue to give, you will reap the harvest in due course.

My life and ministry involves a constant giving out to others. I do not begrudge that at all because it is a privilege to serve the King of kings, and humbling to be used by Him to speak into others' lives. But I cannot deny there are times when I become exceedingly weary. There are so many demands, even when I feel there is nothing left to give.

And yet the Lord always supplies the resources of energy necessary under the anointing of the Holy Spirit. I hear this word in my own heart, never to become weary in doing good. There will be ample time to rest in heaven – I trust!

The message is clear. **Do not give up. Do not compromise in the matter of expressing your love in giving to God and to others.** Give time to prayer and study of the Word. Faith will be enlarged and you will reap the rewards of faith.

> Therefore, as we have opportunity, let us do good to all people, especially to those who belong to the family of believers. (Gal. 6:10)

You can have victory over selfishness by taking the opportunities to give which God places before you. Sometimes this will require an act of faith because you feel inadequate or fear that you will lose rather than gain. At such times you have to believe God's Word – not the world, your own flesh or the devil.

Your key to a victorious life:
   KEEP GIVING TO THE LORD AND OTHERS.

22

Victory in Sickness

The way to victory:
   Allowing God to use sickness creatively for His purpose
   gives victory *in* sickness.

Your victory scripture:
   Surely he took up our infirmities and carried our
   sorrows. (Isa. 53:4)

GOD'S ANSWER TO SICKNESS

There is a difference between victory *in* sickness and
victory *over* sickness.

Without sin there would be no sickness; both are
consequences of man's fallen nature. In the Old Testament
it is clear that God does not want His people to be ill,
although He allows plagues and sickness to overtake them
if they are persistent in their disobedience and rebellion.
For the same reasons He allows their enemies to defeat
them. Any amount of suffering and hardship would be
worthwhile to bring them back to obedience to His
covenant with them. Then He would bless them mightily
and abundantly, which is what He desired.

The Lord wants to bless His people, not to curse them.
Satan is the agent of sickness, as we see in the book of Job.
It was the enemy, not the Lord, who attacked Job in many
ways, including sickness.

The prophecy of Isaiah looks forward to what God will effect through the Cross, when the new covenant would be ratified with the blood of His Son. Jesus dealt with every spiritual, emotional and physical condition.

Surely he took up our infirmities and carried our sorrows . . . and by his wounds we are healed. (Isa. 53:4–5)

He suffered, spirit, soul and body, to bring salvation, or health, to spirit, soul and body.

THE CROSS AND SICKNESS

Below are phrases from the prophecy of Isaiah 52:13–53:12 describing the various ways in which Jesus suffered. The righthand column shows how people can identify with different aspects of Jesus' work of total salvation.

WHAT JESUS SUFFERED	THOSE WHO IDENTIFY WITH HIM
His appearance was so disfigured beyond that of any man and his form marred beyond human likeness.	Those who are born with physical defect, or who are maimed.
He had no beauty or majesty to attract us to him, nothing in his appearance that we should desire him.	Those who consider they lack any beauty or attraction – either physically or as people.
He was despised and rejected by men.	All who feel despised and have been rejected by others.
A man of sorrows.	All who have experienced personal sorrow.
Familiar with suffering.	Those who have continual suffering.

WHAT JESUS SUFFERED	THOSE WHO IDENTIFY WITH HIM
He was despised.	Those who know what it is to be hated.
Surely he took up our infirmities.	Any who experience sickness, emotional or physical.
And carried our sorrows.	All who are grief-stricken.
We considered him stricken by God, smitten by him, and afflicted.	All in the prime of life who are struck down with sickness.
He was pierced for our transgressions.	All who sin.
He was crushed for our iniquities.	All those who feel crushed by the weight of their sin and guilt.
The punishment that brought us peace was upon him.	All who deserve to be punished and judged by God.
By his wounds we are healed.	Any who are sick can receive the healing which He accomplished.
He was oppressed.	All who are oppressed can be set free.
Afflicted.	All who suffer affliction, no matter what its nature.
By oppression and judgment he was taken away.	All who are oppressed and judged falsely.
For the transgressions of my people he was stricken.	All who deserve punishment for their sins.
He was assigned a grave with the wicked.	All who deserve death can now receive the gospel of eternal life.
It was the Lord's will to crush him.	What love the Father must have for you, to crush His Son on your behalf!

WHAT JESUS SUFFERED	THOSE WHO IDENTIFY WITH HIM
And cause him to suffer.	To deliver you from suffering.
The will of the Lord will prosper in his hand.	His will is that you should have life in all its fullness.
He poured out his life unto death.	Through His death you have received that life.

VICTORY IN JESUS' MINISTRY

Healing of physical disease played a major part in Jesus' ministry. These healings were seen as signs that Jesus had come with the good news of God's Kingdom. They demonstrated that His Kingdom is more powerful and has greater authority than anything that can be perpetrated by the dominion of darkness.

Matthew clearly states that healing of sickness and deliverance from demons were a fulfilment of the Isaiah prophecy:

> When evening came, many who were demon-possessed were brought to him, and he drove out the spirits with a word and healed all the sick. This was to fulfil what was spoken through the prophet Isaiah, 'He took up our infirmities and carried our diseases' (Matt. 8:16–17)

How could Matthew apply these verses to what happened in Jesus' ministry *before* the Cross? **What Jesus did in a limited time during the three years or so of His human ministry was made eternally available to all men of all ages of all nations, who put their faith in Him, when He went to the Cross.**

Jesus took away the infirmities and diseases of those who came to Him in faith during His earthly ministry.

Jesus takes away the infirmities and diseases of those who come to Him now in faith, because He has dealt with their need on the Cross.

By the power of His Spirit we can therefore see and experience the same works as Jesus did. He came and waged war on sin and sickness and was victorious over both. In the name of Jesus that victory is made available to all.

VICTORY IN SICKNESS

In an ideal, perfect world there would be neither sin nor sickness. Until Jesus comes again such a perfect world will not exist. Every person sins and it is possible for anyone to be sick.

This does not mean God *wants* you to be sick, just as He never *wants* you to sin.

As you are in Christ, there is no condemnation for you if you sin. You can receive forgiveness through the Lord's grace and mercy.

There is certainly no condemnation for you if you become sick. Although some sickness is the direct result of sin, this is by no means always the case. The enemy often attacks with sickness, as he did with Job.

Healing for any and every disease is possible through Jesus. With God nothing is impossible, and 'Everything is possible for him who believes' (Mark 9:23). And yet it needs to be clearly stated that **a Christian who does not receive healing is not condemned.**

Many have testified to how God has met them in sickness. They speak of important refining and spiritual developments taking place in their lives in times of sickness. There can be no doubt that such testimonies are genuine. However there is no lesson God teaches us in sickness that He would not rather teach us in health. The

Lord does not want to make us sick in order to teach us. What kind of a father would do that to his children?

When ill, people have time to reflect, to be still, to listen and respond to what the Lord may have been saying for some time. The person may have been unwilling or unable to hear because of his ceaseless activity or preoccupation with other things. There is nothing like pain to encourage repentance and a crying out to God. In such times people become aware of their need to re-order the priorities in their lives.

If the time of illness is used creatively for God's purposes, then it could certainly be claimed that the Christian has experienced spiritual victory *in* sickness. He has come to a renewed repentance and submission of his life to God.

CRIPPLING DISEASES

And yet there is another way of understanding victory *in* sickness. Prolonged sickness, disfigurement, crippling diseases and maiming accidents can all cause deep emotional hurt, resentment and bitterness, mixed with a sense of non-acceptance by others. In other words, instead of the sickness being creative it is destructive, not only of the body but of the person. This may be an understandable reaction among non-Christians, but should not be the case among God's redeemed people.

Sickness must not be allowed to overcome the personality; the person must overcome the sickness. Many Christians have been brought through to such victory. They may be paralysed, bedridden or confined to a wheel-chair, they may have been born with crippling disfigurement, but they show no sign of resentment, bitterness or hatred even towards those who may have caused the disaster. They bear no malice towards God who is well aware of their predicament. Instead their lives are shining examples of those who know the love and acceptance of Jesus. They are an encouragement to other Christians because, despite their disfigurement, His love and graciousness shine out of their lives.

The sickness has not triumphed over their human spirits. In their spirits they have triumphed over the sickness. This in itself is a great work of God's Spirit within them and we can be thankful for their witness and example.

Having experienced this much, some are content to accept the sickness as being God's will for them. They appear to have no faith that they could, or should, be completely restored physically, even though they know such things are possible and do happen today. They have victory *in* their sickness, but not *over* the sickness itself.

COMPLETE HEALING

Others are not content with victory in their sickness. They are reaching out to God for complete healing and deliverance from their need. They believe for this and nothing less. They may need first to be set free from any sense of bitterness or resentment for their situation, or receive victory *in* their sickness. **But they look to God for the Word of faith which will restore them to complete health.**

The Lord honours such faith today and many mighty miracles take place as a result. The fact that they occur more readily in Third World countries may be significant. Perhaps there is a simplicity of faith in Jesus to effect the miracle. Perhaps it is not enough to know victory *in* sickness if there is no welfare state to care for you. There is no greater incentive to faith than to know the Lord is the only answer, rather than being one course among a number of different options.

Jesus certainly brought people victory over sickness. He was not content to comfort people in their need; He met their need. This is surely His purpose today.

We can praise God for those who experience victory *in*

sickness. But we can reach out to God with the faith which will bring victory *over* sickness.

However, do not belittle the work of God's grace in those who have met with Him in their sickness. And do not imagine you will need to become sick for God to teach you.

You are a disciple of Jesus.
Sit at His feet and learn from Him.
Respond readily to His Word and the leading of His Spirit.
Be quick to learn and respond, in health or sickness.

Your key to a victorious life:
SICKNESS WILL NOT TRIUMPH OVER YOU.

23

Victory over Sickness

The way to victory:
   Understand that the Lord does not want you to be sick;
   He wants you to be whole in spirit, soul and body.

Your victory scripture:
   By his wounds we are healed. (Isa. 53:5)

HEAL THE SICK

Because the Cross of Jesus embraced every healing need, He wants you to experience healing *over* sickness as well as other adverse circumstances.

In the New Testament, there is a clear distinction between suffering and sickness. We are called to suffer for the sake of the Kingdom. This may involve persecution, rejection, even physical deprivation and torture. We are called to suffer the cost of self-denial, to take up our personal crosses day by day and follow Jesus.

We are not called to be sick.

Jesus would not have given His disciples power and authority to heal the sick if His Father had caused the sickness or willed it. God is not divided against Himself in this way.

Healing goes with the proclamation of the good news of God's Kingdom. As disciples of Jesus today we have inherited this commission.

He called his twelve disciples to him and gave them authority to drive out evil spirits and to heal every disease and sickness . . . As you go, preach this message: 'The kingdom of heaven is near.' Heal the sick, raise the dead, cleanse those who have leprosy, drive out demons. Freely you have received, freely give. (Matt. 10:1,7–8)

The Acts of the Apostles makes it clear that these men continued to fulfil this commission after Jesus' death and resurrection, when the Holy Spirit had come upon them.

RESIST SICKNESS

It is God's plan for His Church to extend healing to the sick in the name of Jesus. Likewise, **He desires His children to stand against sickness, as they are called to stand against sin.**

God's best purpose is that you should not be sick. If sickness attacks you He wants you to stand against it in the name of Jesus, refusing to accept it. This is a very different attitude from quietly submitting to sickness as being God's will for you.

You may need to speak to the sickness. Jesus tells you to speak to mountains commanding them to be moved, not doubting in your heart that they will be moved.

You can accept and believe symptoms or you can come against them in faith. When you resist them, the early symptoms disappear and the disease does not take hold of you. The best method of defence is attack! You may experience a period of conflict, as if a battle is going on within you. But as you persist in faith you come through to victory.

The medical profession today confirms what the Bible has affirmed for centuries. The majority of physical sicknesses are psychosomatic; they begin in the mind. The Christian can go further and say that the mind is often in turmoil because the person's spiritual life is in turmoil.

Keep your mind clear of thoughts of sickness, of fears of becoming ill. Those who dread sickness are not surprised when they become ill. Their expectations are fulfilled. Those who dwell on symptoms will see them intensify. Often physical pain is the result of emotional and mental anguish.

Often people seek healing of a physical complaint, and discover that God wants first to deal with the anguish and tension within them. There is little point in removing the symptoms if the cause remains.

WHOLENESS

Jesus met your every need on the Cross, spiritual, emotional, psychological and physical. When coming to God with faith you need to appreciate that He wants you to have victory over the sickness. **He has not created you to be sick, but to be made whole through Jesus.**

He usually starts with the heart and works outwards, even though there are many occasions when you would like Him to do the reverse. But He is concerned with your total well-being, with 'wholeness', health of spirit, soul and body. **In coming to Him for healing come with your whole being, not part of yourself. It is *you* He wants to heal, not only some part of your body.**

Above all He wants you to live in peace, to have faith in Him and walk in His ways so that you do not become vulnerable to sickness because of fear, tension and worry.

Disobedience can lead to sickness. The obvious examples are certain sexually-related diseases, and those caused by overwork and over-indulgence. So Christians need to see that their lives are regulated according to God's Word.

If heart strain is caused by overweight, which is caused by greed, it is obvious that the Lord will want to deal with the greed and whatever causes the greed. This may be the sin of over-indulgence; it may be that the person is eating in an attempt to provide some emotional compensation.

Because of His love for the person, Jesus wants to deal with the root cause so there can be true victory over every area of dis-ease.

RECEIVE YOUR HEALING

There are many ways in which the believer can receive healing. This is not the place for a lengthy discussion of this subject, but we can take note of a few important principles.

1 Do not allow the sickness into your heart. If you believe in the sickness you will not have faith to see it removed from your body. This does not mean that you refuse to acknowledge the existence of the sickness. But you do not regard the illness as the ultimate truth, which is the healing that is part of your inheritance in Christ.

2 Your faith is in the victory of Jesus: 'By his wounds you are healed.'

3 As you pray, see your healing as an established fact. You are taking hold of that which is already done in Christ.

4 Do not be double-minded about the subject. It is the Lord's will to heal you.

5 Speak to the sickness in the name of Jesus, commanding it to leave you. He tells you not to doubt the outcome.

6 As you pray, believe you have received your healing. 'Whatever you ask for in prayer, believe that you have received it, and it will be yours' (Mark 11:24).

7 Having prayed with faith, you are walking in God's healing not in sickness.

8 Before asking the Lord to deal with the physical condition, be sure you are right with Him spiritually. Ask Him to forgive your sins, and be specific when you do so.

9 Be sure that you have forgiven others, that you are not holding on to any hurt, bitterness or resentment.

10 If necessary, ask others to pray with you in the name of Jesus. Believe such times as being occasions when you actually receive from God, whether or not you are conscious of any particular sensation.

It is important to have the right faith attitudes. The method by which you receive the healing is unimportant. **Do not look to men,** even those with a reputation for being used in healing. **Look directly to the Lord Jesus.**

    Put your faith in Him.
    You will receive your healing in His name.

Jesus has won the victory over sickness; so Jesus can give you that victory in your circumstances.

Faith comes from hearing God's word in your heart. Even if faith does not exist at first, God can speak His Word to your heart by His Spirit. Such a word does not lead to a general sense that the healing will happen sometime in the future. The Lord may give such a promise that it is His will to heal. **But promises have to be appropriated by faith. A specific word from God leads to specific action. When He speaks that Word, believe what He says.**

When you know in your spirit it is done, the matter is resolved. The physical sickness may disappear immediately, or begin to go at that moment. Sometimes there can be a time delay in the manifestation of healing. However, **at that moment of faith you know the matter is resolved.** You are in the Lord's hands and He does not fail.

You can appropriate emotional healing in the same way.

Appreciate that Jesus has met your need. It is His desire and intention to free you from that need.

He has taken your sin.
He has suffered your sorrow and rejection.
He has carried your sicknesses to the Cross.
By His wounds you are healed.

Your key to a victorious life:
    RESIST SICKNESS IN THE NAME OF JESUS.[1]

[1] For a fuller treatment of the subject of healing, see Colin Urquhart, *Receive Your Healing* (Hodder 1986).

24

Victory over Oppression

The way to victory:
   Do not allow your spiritual ear to be dulled to God's voice because you listen instead to the enemy's lies.

Your victory scripture:
   It is for freedom that Christ has set us free. (Gal. 5:1)

BELIEVING YOUR INHERITANCE

'The devil is oppressing me.' Certainly the devil will try to oppress God's people. But if believers exercise the faith and authority they are given he will not be successful in his attempts.

Everything in God's Kingdom is positive. In His Kingdom there are certain clearly defined principles by which God works.

The devil is unprincipled and attempts to contradict the positive with his negatives.

The Spirit gives freedom. The devil tries to steal this from the believer by tempting him to disbelieve his inheritance or focus his attention on his fears, feelings and failures instead of on the truth.

The mind is usually his first line of attack. He sows a negative thought. If this is received he follows it with another and another. The Christian is accepting a negative line of thought which affects his whole attitude to some aspect of his life.

Take sickness as an example. The first thought may be: 'You have cancer.' If this is received it will not be long before the devil points to any unusual bodily sensation as being the first evidences of the disease. He may continue his subtle tactics by suggesting: 'There is a history of cancer in your family, isn't there?' 'This is the age your cousin died of cancer.' And so on.

He will say anything to encourage fear and cause the person to believe he is really going to die of this disease. His business is destruction.

Of course, the devil will do similar things in many other areas of life besides sickness, encouraging you to fear the future, to believe the worst is going to happen, that you will inevitably fail in whatever lies ahead of you.

His most destructive attacks are those made on the principles of your faith, contradicting the truth of God's word.

Through His blood you are accepted by Jesus. Satan will suggest you are unacceptable and will point to your sins and inadequacies as evidence of his contention.

Where you repent the Lord forgives your sins. Satan will want you to think that forgiveness cannot be that simple, that you deserved to be punished for your sins.

You live in Christ. The enemy will point out your failures again and again, suggesting you are so unworthy you could not possibly live in Jesus.

Christ lives in you. The devil will encourage you to believe the Lord would not come to live in someone so unholy. It cannot be true.

Christ leads you in His triumphant procession. Satan suggests this is the biggest joke of the century with your record of failures.

You are made worthy in God's sight. The enemy points to every sin as evidence of your unworthiness. And so on.

Every attack is calculated to cause unbelief, confusion, condemnation and failure, by denying the truth.

Never is the devil more active, it seems, than when you
need to hear directly from God about a certain matter.
How many people admit to finding it difficult to discern the
voice of God from the deceptions of the evil one?

The answer to these attacks is simple and obvious. **You
hold on to the truth and refuse to accept any of the lying
deceptions of the enemy.** This requires constant vigilance,
for he is likely to strike like the serpent he is, at the most
unlikely moment.

PERSONAL ATTACK

Oppression can take different forms. There are the times
when your personal worth and faith seem under attack.
The devil wants you to believe you are a no-good, spiritual
failure, that God does not want anything to do with you. He
suggests you have failed so miserably even your ultimate
salvation is far from certain or secure.

If you listen to him you lose all your confidence before
God and then feel trapped by your circumstances. Everything seems hopeless, you feel helpless and the Lord seems
far removed from your concerns.

An extreme form of this state causes depression. The
person has believed so many lies, and has thus become so
negative in his thinking, he no longer knows how to be
positive. His eyes are not on the truth of the Word, but on
himself and his feelings. **He loses sight of the victory because
his eyes are on himself instead of the Victor.**

The one who has become depressed by believing so many
lies will need to recognise the folly of what he has been
doing in listening to the enemy. He will have to repent of
this, claiming God's forgiveness and the freedom He alone
can give.

Then he will also need to have his mind renewed. This
is a process rather than something which happens in a
moment of time. He will need to fill his mind with the

positive truth of the Word. **Listening to the enemy will have made his spiritual ear dull to the voice of the Holy Spirit.**

I find I have to be constantly vigilant, so that the enemy is not allowed to establish a negative foothold anywhere in my thinking. I know that I cannot be sensitive to what God is saying if I allow my mind to be filled with Satan's lies.

THE FATHER OF LIES

The other way in which the enemy will try to undermine your faith is by pointing to the difficult circumstances in which you are sometimes placed. He will suggest every problem is an indication that God cannot truly love you, or He would not have allowed such things to happen. The irony is that the devil has been responsible for the very things for which he wants to blame God. But Satan always seems to play the same tunes; so they are easily recognisable.

'Why should this have happened to you if God really loves you?'
'This must be punishment for your sins.'
'Faith may work for others, but it would never work for you.'
'How can a God of love allow you to be sick?'
'How can God possibly love you, when you suffer so much pain?'
'He cannot be much of a God if he is with you always and yet you experience so much rejection and confusion.'

He nags away persistently with such lies. So you have to deny them just as persistently.

Hold on to the truth.
If you resist the devil, he will flee from you.
Refuse to accept any of his negative lies or accusations.
Take the shield of faith, which repels all his attacks.

It is easy to tell the voice of the devil if you remember:

He accuses you; Jesus does not.
He tries to condemn you; Jesus does not.
He undermines faith; Jesus gives faith.
He diverts your attention on to the problems; the Holy
     Spirit directs you to Jesus.
He blames God; Jesus offers help.
He is negative; the Father, Jesus and the Holy Spirit are
     positive.

YOU ARE FREE

You can expect the devil to oppose you, but you do not
need to allow him to oppress you, to make you feel that
either he or your circumstances are on top of you.

Another way in which you can experience the enemy's
attempts to oppress is through a sense of spiritual heaviness
coming on you. You may feel very tired and restless,
unable to concentrate for no accountable reason, especially
when you have important Kingdom business in hand. You
may find it difficult to look to the Lord in prayer, and praise
is exceedingly difficult.

**At such times take authority in the name of Jesus over the
devil and all his works. Claim the victory that is yours and
praise Jesus.** This may require a real act of the will at first,
but as you persevere so you will break right through to the
glory of Jesus' majesty.

Oppression is like ropes with which the devil wants to
bind you. You are created to be free in Christ Jesus, not
bound. So do not let yourself be bound.

> **It is for freedom that Christ has set us free. Stand firm,
> then, and do not let yourselves be burdened again by a
> yoke of slavery. (Gal. 5:1)**

The enemy even tries to oppress through religious activity.
He wants to limit the freedom of the Holy Spirit among

God's people, through tradition, conformity and legalism. Paul's message to the Galatians is clear and is certainly relevant today.

The cause of the gospel is damaged severely by religious prejudice, self-righteousness, denominationalism and judgmental attitudes towards other believers. It is not always understood who is stoking the fires of division or who encourages attitudes which oppose the liberty of God's Spirit in churches.

Do not listen to the enemy's attempts to encourage a return to religious conformity and tradition.

Do not allow him to put you back under the bondage of the law.

He will do anything to take away the freedom you have in Jesus.

It is for freedom Christ has set you free in every area of your life.

Your key to a victorious life:
CHRIST HAS SET YOU FREE TO LIVE IN FREEDOM.

25

Victory over Error

The way to victory:
   **Check against God's Word your ideas and reason, your
   feelings and decisions, and what others teach you.**

Your victory scripture:
   **I tell you the truth, if anyone keeps my word, he will
   never see death. (John. 8:51)**

THE TRUTH

The enemy wants to distort the truth. The greatest danger
for Christians comes from ignorance of the truth.

Many admit they need a better knowledge and understanding of God's Word. Intention or desire is not enough.
The only way to combat error is with the truth.

**You need to know the truth of what God has done for you
   in Jesus.**
You need to know who you are as a child of God.
**You need to know the rich inheritance you have through
   His grace.**
**You need to know God's purpose for your life and what
   He expects of you.**

The Lord speaks to you personally through His Word and
by His Spirit. The Holy Spirit is the Spirit of truth who will
guide you with the truth.

Just as light penetrates and overcomes darkness, so truth overcomes error. **Truth is not a matter of debate or discussion. Truth is truth and never changes.** The truth of God and His Son, Jesus, is eternal. This is why Jesus says that heaven and earth will pass away, but His words will never pass away.

To live by faith is to live by the truth. And the truth is often stranger than the facts we experience with our senses.

I TELL YOU THE TRUTH

Everything Jesus says is truth. But sometimes He used the phrase 'I tell you the truth' because He knew the statement that followed would meet with unbelief. Jesus is saying that this is definitely the truth whether you believe it or not.

As we look at some of these statements from John's gospel, we can appreciate that such truth is rejected by many today, even by some who call themselves Christians. They argue against these truths with their reason, or question what Jesus says because the truth offends their own ideas of what they want to do with their lives.

I tell you the truth, no-one can see the kingdom of God unless he is born again. (John 3:3)

I tell you the truth, no-one can enter the kingdom of God unless he is born of water and the Spirit. (John 3:5)

Many of these statements relate to who will receive the gift of eternal life and go to heaven. These truths cut right across popular misconceptions that everyone will go to heaven.

I tell you the truth, whoever hears my word and believes him who sent me has eternal life and will not be condemned; he has crossed over from death to life. (John 5:24)

Note the emphasis on personal faith in Jesus; he who believes has eternal life.

You have received the gift of eternal life.
You will not be condemned.
You have crossed over from death to life.
You have been born again.
You have repented and come to personal faith in Jesus.
You know Him as your Lord and Saviour.
You are born of water and the spirit.

Without Jesus you could not have God's life within you. Because you know and love Him you can feed on His words, for He is the living Bread which has come down from heaven.

I tell you the truth, unless you can eat the flesh of the Son of Man and drink his blood, you have no life in you. Whoever eats my flesh and drinks my blood has eternal life, and I will raise him up at the last day. (John 6:53–54)

The blood of Jesus cleanses you from your sins. You belong to Him; and He is the resurrection and the life. And so you have His assurance that you will not die eternally, but He will raise you up to be with Him in triumph.

I tell you the truth, everyone who sins is a slave to sin. Now a slave has no permanent place in the family, but a son belongs to it for ever. So if the Son sets you free, you will be free indeed. (John 8:34–36)

You are no longer a slave but a son, by faith in Jesus Christ.
You have the rights and privileges of a Son of God's Kingdom.
You also have the responsibility of a son, not to be ruled by sin but to walk in loving and faithful obedience to your heavenly Father.

The Son has set you free from sin, from your past, from hurt, rejection and bitterness.

It is His truth that has set you free –
from the devil
from yourself
from every bondage.

'If you hold to my teaching, you are really my disciples. Then you will know the truth, and the truth will set you free' (John 8:31–32).

Jesus gives you mighty promises as you live His Word:

I tell you the truth, if anyone keeps my word, he will never see death. (John 8:51)

Jesus is the only way to the Father. No one can receive the gift of the Kingdom except through Him:

I tell you the truth, I am the gate for the sheep. All who ever came before me were thieves and robbers, but the sheep did not listen to them. I am the gate; whoever enters through me will be saved. (John 10:7–8)

The cost of belonging to the Kingdom is that you follow Jesus' example. Like a seed you must fall into the ground and die to self, to what you have been, in order that you might be fruitful for God and enjoy His eternal reward.

I tell you the truth, unless a grain of wheat falls to the ground and dies, it remains only a single seed. But if it dies, it produces many seeds. The man who loves his life will lose it, while the man who hates his life in this world will keep it for eternal life. (John 12:24–25)

As true disciples we are to be like our Master, not having exalted ideas about ourselves, but walking humbly before Him and others.

I tell you the truth, no servant is greater than his master, nor is a messenger greater than the one who sent him.

Now that you know these things, you will be blessed if you do them. (John 13:16–17)

Jesus submitted to the principle of dying to Himself, and He came the Servant of all. We are sent out and commissioned in His name, and Jesus makes this amazing statement about us as His representatives or ambassadors.

I tell you the truth, whoever accepts anyone I send accepts me; and whoever accepts me accepts the one who sent me. (John 13:20)

You go in Jesus' name, to proclaim His truth in the power of His Spirit, in the face of the error, misunderstanding and unbelief which abound in the world around you.

Even more amazing is what Jesus tells us is possible when we go in faith:

I tell you the truth, anyone who has faith in me will do what I have been doing. He will do even greater things than these, because I am going to the Father. (John 14:12)

THE EFFECTS OF THE TRUTH

These are only a small number of the challenging things Jesus said as He revealed the truth.

The truth opens the way for you to eternal life and God's Kingdom.

The truth frees you from condemnation and leads you to fullness of life.

The truth leads to resurrection and glory.

The truth proclaims your Sonship through God's grace.

The truth points you to the only Saviour and Lord, showing you all He has done for you to set you free from every bondage.

The truth shows you the cost of discipleship and the way to be fruitful in God.

The truth gives you your commission and God's promises.

The truth is Jesus Himself.

The truth sets you free.

It is not the truth of yourself that will give you victory, but the truth of all Jesus has done for you, and what God has made you now you belong to Him.

This truth will correct any error about the way you view yourself, your circumstances or your future. The truth will keep you from error concerning the nature of God Himself or His purpose for you.

Anyone who runs ahead and does not continue in the teaching of Christ does not have God; whoever continues in the teaching has both the Father and the Son. (2 John 9)

Check your ideas and reason against the Word of God. Do not accept anything that is not in line with the scriptures.

Check what others teach against God's revealed truth. Do not accept anything which is a contradiction to His Word, no matter how plausible or even 'loving' it may seem.

Check your feelings and decisions against the truth. When inconsistent with the Word, deny the feelings and reject the thoughts you have. **Make choices in line with God's words and then you will walk in His way and fulfil His will.**

Your key to a victorious life:

LIVE BY THE TRUTH OF GOD'S WORD.

26

Victory over Temptation

The way to victory:
    Jesus can help you to be victorious over every temptation.

Your victory scripture:
    Because he himself suffered when he was tempted, he is able to help those who are being tempted. (Heb. 2:18)

TEMPTATION IN JESUS' MINISTRY

No matter what temptation you experience, Jesus is present with you. He knows what it is like from His own experience to have to stand firm under similar temptation.

Because he himself suffered when he was tempted, he is able to help those who are being tempted. (Heb. 2:18)

This is the extent to which the Son of God identified with your situation. With the Lord on your side and His Spirit within, you are able to resist and overcome the temptation.

For we do not have a high priest who is unable to sympathise with our weaknesses, but we have one who has been tempted in every way, just as we are – yet was without sin. (Heb. 4:15)

Jesus was always victorious and He can enable you to resist temptation in whatever form it occurs. He understands your weaknesses; He knows your vulnerability and the things you find difficult. This does not imply that He condones sin, but He is present to enable you to withstand the temptation and demonstrate your faithfulness and love for Him by your obedience to His will.

> Blessed is the man who perseveres under trial, because when he has stood the test, he will receive the crown of life that God has promised to those who love him. (Jas. 1:12)

During his manhood, Jesus was tempted in every way, yet remained sinless because He resisted all temptation. Before His public ministry began, the devil tempted Him to act independently of His Father, to take the initiative for His life into His own hands. This Jesus refused to do.

He underwent many further attacks, but none greater than the conflict He experienced in the Garden of Gethsemane. We cannot imagine the spiritual and mental anguish He experienced which caused Him to sweat blood. We can only be thankful that He made the decision He did. Lovingly and humbly He submitted His will to that of His Father, 'Not my will, but yours be done' (Luke 22:42).

TEMPTATION IN YOUR LIFE

It is not a sin to be tempted. What you do in response to the temptation is what matters. It can come at any time, even when you least expect it:

> If you think you are standing firm, be careful that you don't fall! No temptation has seized you except what is common to man. And God is faithful; he will not let you be tempted beyond what you can bear. But when you are tempted, he will also provide a way out so that you can stand up under it. (1 Cor. 10:12–13)

Paul is making a number of important points here:

1 'Pride comes before a fall' often proves true. For pride leads to complacency and a lack of watchfulness. Then a person is vulnerable to temptation. Even when you are standing firm you need to be on the watch.

2   Whatever temptation you suffer is experienced by many others. It may seem unique to you, but the devil plays the same cards again and again, because he knows the weak, vulnerable points at which to attack.

3   You can be sure the Lord will never allow you to 'be tempted beyond what you can bear'. He does not want to see you fall from grace. He is the Lord who is able to keep you from falling and present you blameless before His throne.

4   No matter what the temptation, the Lord will always provide you with an escape route. So it is not right to say: 'I couldn't help it. I felt I had to do it.' The honest truth is that you chose to sin. It is a sign of God's faithfulness to you as His covenant child that He will not allow Satan to attack you in such a way that you have to yield to his demands.

5   You are able to withstand the temptation; you can be victorious. Why give Satan the satisfaction of even a minor victory?

James gives us further truths:

> When tempted, no-one should say, 'God is tempting me.' For God cannot be tempted by evil, nor does he tempt anyone; but each one is tempted when, by his own evil desire, he is dragged away and enticed. Then, after desire has conceived, it gives birth to sin; and sin, when it is full-grown, gives birth to death. (Jas. 1:13–15)

6   The devil is the tempter, not God. He allows the enemy to tempt because temptation exposes your vulnerable areas. You see the ways in which you need to trust God, and be built up in His strength. But God Himself does not tempt you. He wants you to stand firm in faith against the temptation.

7   Temptation does not create sin; it simply exposes the sinful desires which exist within you. It exposes what is in your heart; those things which are alien to God's purposes but which you still desire; your 'own evil desires'.

8 If you allow evil desires to entice you away from God's purposes, you will inevitably sin. Satan offers all kinds of temporary pleasures, many of which are illusory. **Jesus offers eternal rewards to those who remain faithful to Him.**

SPIRIT AND FLESH

Your flesh will always be flesh, and can never be anything other than flesh. Satan wants you to go back to the flesh. Jesus wants you to walk in the Spirit. You have authority over the devil; so do not allow him to seduce or deceive you.

It is important therefore to nip the problem in the bud. **Resist the first sinful thought or desire. Do not dwell on the matter. The more you concentrate on it, perhaps enjoying the mental anticipation of the sin, the more difficult it will be to resist.**

You may not want to resist because you desire the object of the temptation so much. If you yield you may be temporarily satisfied in the flesh, but you will suffer spiritual defeat. **If you resist the temptation, you will experience victory over the flesh, reckoning yourself dead to your own desires and able to please the Lord.**

To dwell on the thought of the sin is to invite the sin itself. The thought is as bad as the deed, Jesus tells us. But He does not imply there is any condemnation in the fact that we are tempted. He was tempted in the wilderness, but did not sin because He immediately rebuffed the devil.

Even when you do yield to temptation, deliberately or unintentionally, the Lord is still ready to restore you through His forgiving love. But remember He is 'able to keep you from falling and to present you before his glorious presence without fault and with great joy' (Jude 24).

Remember: **temptation is not sin.** Do not be surprised

that you are tempted, or imagine that you will ever reach a point beyond temptation.

Satan's appeal is to the flesh, to the natural self-life. He suggests you satisfy your bodily appetites through sexual immorality, greed or laziness. He tempts you to satisfy yourself, to exalt self, to be self-sufficient and independent. He wants you to lie, deceive, cheat. In other words he wants to reproduce his own distorted character in you because he is utterly opposed to God's purpose of forming Himself in you.

Remember the simple test: Satan will want you to be negative – to refuse to forgive, to judge, condemn, ridicule, destroy. **Jesus will produce the positive nature of His Kingdom life in you by the power of His Spirit.**

It is obviously foolish to put yourself in situations where you know you will be open to temptation. Your flesh will always be flesh and can never become spiritual. **The way to deal with the flesh is to reckon it dead, crucified with Christ.**

Instead of getting worried about fleshly desire, you can adopt the attitude: 'That's my flesh. Praise God I have died to all that nonsense and do not have to yield. My trust is in the Lord. Glory be to Jesus.' You will find that such tactics are far more effective than being full of concern because you have detected some ungodly desire.

When others fall into sin, do not adopt a judgmental attitude, no matter how grievous the situation may seem. Rather than be critical of others, you are warned to 'watch yourself, or you also may be tempted' (Gal. 6:1).

Never become complacent. You are not beyond temptation, which can come in unexpected ways at unexpected times. When it happens, **resist and walk in victory.**

Your key to a victorious life:
WALK IN THE SPIRIT; SAY 'NO' TO EVERY TEMPTATION TO INDULGE THE FLESH.

27

Victory over Pride

The way to victory:
  Submit yourself to God, delighting to do whatever He asks of you, no matter how insignificant.

Your victory scripture:
  God opposes the proud but gives grace to the humble. (Prov. 3:34; Jas. 4:6; 1 Pet. 5:5)

JESUS' HUMILITY

Jesus said: 'I am gentle and humble in heart' (Matt. 11:29). It is difficult to imagine the love which lay behind the Creator of the universe choosing to be born in the weakness of human flesh as a fragile child.

Imagine God walking on earth, tending the needs of His people, teaching them the truth, encouraging them to receive His gifts and inherit His promises! The Son of God even washes His disciples' feet, doing the work of a humble slave.

Jesus came to reveal the Father, not to glorify Himself.

My food is to do the will of him who sent me and to finish his work. (John 4:34)

I tell you the truth, the Son can do nothing by himself; he can do only what he sees his Father doing, because whatever the Father does the Son also does. (John 5:19)

179

> By myself I can do nothing; I judge only as I hear, and my
> judgment is just, for I seek not to please myself but
> him who sent me. (John 5:30)

**Here is the secret of Jesus' success, of His ability to manifest
perfectly the love, power, and authority of God. He was not
interested in doing what He wanted for Himself. His delight
was in pleasing His Father and fulfilling His purpose.**

> For I have come down from heaven not to do my will but
> to do the will of him who sent me. (John 6:38)

> I do nothing on my own but speak just what the Father
> has taught me. (John 8:28)

> The one who sent me is with me; he has not left me alone,
> for I always do what pleases him. (John 8:29)

The Anointed One submitting himself to rejection, humi-
liation, torture and crucifixion, all in obedience to His
Father's will. What love! What humility!

YOUR ATTITUDE

> Your attitude should be the same as that of Christ Jesus:
> Who, being in very nature God, did not consider equality
> with God something to be grasped, but made himself
> nothing, taking the very nature of a servant, being made
> in human likeness. (Phil. 2:5–7)

He sowed His life, letting the seed fall into the ground and
die, that there might be a mighty harvest of souls in God's
heavenly Kingdom. Without that sowing there would not
be the reaping.

'Your attitude should be the same,' says Paul. Being
prepared to die to self, to be made nothing in the world's
eyes, in order that you might be fruitful for God.

This is the death and resurrection principle that has to be
seen in our lives. There is no glory without the Cross.

The Lord gave me a picture of packets of seeds on a shelf.

The packets represented churches and the seeds the Christians who belong to them. The seeds in these packets were praying for revival. They wanted to see God's glory in the land, with many turning to Him in repentance and faith. It seemed their prayers were having little effect.

These packets needed to be taken from the shelf. The seeds had to fall to the ground and die. Then they could bear fruit. Then there could be a harvest of righteousness in the land.

Can we expect to receive all God wants to give us without being prepared to respond to His Word? The self-life does not want to fall into the ground and die. It will do anything to resist such total commitment, which is why the Church does not experience continual revival.

Pride challenges God.

Pride wants to please self rather than Him.

Pride leads many to contradict God's Word, preferring their own reason and ideas.

Pride ignores the need for spiritual discipline and exalts self.

Pride draws attention to the Christian rather than his Lord, when witnessing or testifying.

Pride causes the believer to want recognition, position, thanks and praise from others.

Pride wants others to know of the Christian's virtues, accomplishments, revelations, healings and miracles.

If the glory is not taken from the Lord at least it is shared by the proud believer, instead of being given exclusively to Jesus. The works of flesh are worth nothing. And the works of the Spirit are just that, the works of the Spirit; and therefore all the glory for them belongs to the Lord.

How many tense and broken relationships in the Church are caused through pride? Through people wanting things to be done according to their personal preferences? Through seeking position, authority, control even, instead

of recognising that the Church is the Lord's and only what
He wants matters.

Even Jesus said: 'If I glorify myself, my glory means
nothing. My Father, whom you claim as your God, is the
one who glorifies me' (John 8:54).

And so James tells us: **'Humble yourselves before the
Lord, and he will lift you up'** (Jas. 4:10). Instead of exalting
yourself, seeking prestige and applause, humble yourself
before God. **'God opposes the proud but gives grace to the
humble.'**

Submit yourself to God and resist the devil's attempts to
stimulate pride. **The way to be victorious over pride is not to
fight the pride but submit yourself to God.**

'Come near to God and he will come near to you' (Jas.
4:8). The arrogant cannot draw near to God. But you can
come into the glory of His holy presence through the Cross.
And the Cross spells the death of the self-life. 'It is no
longer I who live.'

The humility so obvious in Jesus' attitudes comes from
the fact that He knows His right position in relation to the
Father. You can rejoice that you are His child, with all the
attendant privileges and authority. Nevertheless you are to
be a humble and obedient child.

It is necessary to experience the breaking of your pride.
Only by humbling yourself before God, submitting to His
pruning knife, can He cut out of your life what is proud and
vain. He alone can give you the right spirit to be humble
before men.

> The sacrifices of God are a broken spirit; a broken and
> contrite heart, O God, you will not despise. (Ps. 51:17)

Peter also quotes the proverb: **'God opposes the proud but
gives grace to the humble'** (Prov. 3:34; 1 Pet. 5:5). Peter
urges his readers to clothe themselves in humility, to
humble themselves under God's mighty hand that he may
lift them up in due time.

This is a strange way to be victorious. The way up is the

way down! Down on your knees before the mighty and holy one. **The humble one will be more likely to resist temptation, trust God, and be able to exercise His authority and power – like Jesus.**

God actually opposes the proud. You do not want to be in a position where God opposes you. He gives grace to the humble; He gives His everything to those who know they deserve nothing.

Again and again God's Word encourages us to walk humbly before God and man.

The greatest among you will be your servant. (Matt. 23:11)
Whoever exalts himself will be humbled, and whoever humbles himself will be exalted. (Matt. 23:12)
Whoever humbles himself like this child is the greatest in the kingdom of heaven. (Matt. 18:4)
Do not be conceited. (Rom. 12:16)
Clothe yourselves with . . . humility. (Col. 3:12)
Be completely humble and gentle. (Eph. 4:2)
Show true humility towards all men. (Tit. 3:2)

EXALTED IDEAS

Many want to be raised up in ministry, often having exalted ideas about themselves. They say their calling is to be evangelists, although they bring no one to the Lord. They want to be prophets, but no one recognises their anointing. They want to be healers, out of a genuine desire to help people or perhaps to have a publicly acclaimed ministry; but they do not see healings taking place. They even call themselves apostles when this is a calling that can be given only by God, not by a church organisation.

By contrast, others say I am called to serve, called to help, called to quietly give myself.

Those whom God does raise up and use in national and international ministries are those who know His dealings in their lives. They have been humbled and refined, and recognise the need to stay humble before Him. Should pride raise its ugly head and should they ignore the warnings of the Spirit, their ministries can come crashing down about their ears. For those God raises up, He is certainly able to pull down should that prove necessary. He pulls down the proud and haughty but lifts up the humble.

God's dealings with individuals cannot normally be seen. But the fruit is obvious by the people they are and the ministries they have. There are no short cuts to fruitfulness, and no way of avoiding the truth which is so plainly taught in His Word. It is the humble whom God exalts and raises up.

Do you aspire to greater things in God? Do you want to be more fruitful? Do you wish to glorify the Lord more fully in your life?

Then walk in victory over pride, rejoicing that you can prove faithful in little things. The Lord knows you and your deeds. He knows what He can entrust into your hands.

The Father glorified Jesus when He had obediently and faithfully obeyed His commission. Aspire to such humility and obedience. **Your reputation is to be that you are a man or woman of God, that people see Jesus in you – His love, humility and graciousness.** Whatever works of power, the healings and the miracles, you do in His name as a result of His dealings with you, will certainly give Him glory.

If you have any ambition in God, let it be that you grow in true humility. The truly humble man walks in the presence of God, not attempting to do things by His own inspiration or strength, for He recognises the truth of what Jesus says: 'Apart from me you can do nothing' (John 15:5).

Your key to a victorious life:
WALK HUMBLY BEFORE GOD AND OTHERS.

28

Victory over Death

The way to victory:
   If you have died with Christ, you can share in His victory over death and live in resurrection power, with assurance of eternal salvation.

Your victory scripture:
   I am the resurrection and the life . . . whoever lives and believes in me will never die. (John 11:25–26)

RAISED WITH CHRIST

The resurrection demonstrated Jesus' victory over death. He submitted Himself to death that we might have salvation; but death could not hold Him! This was the outworking of His claim before going to the Cross:

I am the resurrection and the life. (John 11:25)

He took all mankind to the Cross that salvation could become possible for any who put their trust in Him. **But it is only those who believe in Him as God's Son who are raised to new life with Him now, and to eventual glory with Him in heaven eternally.**

I am the resurrection and the life. He who believes in me will live, even though he dies; and **whoever lives and believes in me will never die. (John 11:25–26)**

185

The believer will experience a physical death but will not die spiritually. He will share in the victory of Jesus over death. He is in Christ crucified; he is also in Christ risen from the dead. There is a sense, therefore, in which the believer is already seated in heavenly places:

> And God raised us up with Christ and seated us with him in the heavenly realms in Christ Jesus. (Eph. 2:6)

He has done this, Paul tells us, to show 'the incomparable riches of his grace' that He has expressed in His kindness to us in Jesus.

Notice the tense of the verb. 'God raised us up.' It is something that He has done, that is already accomplished because we are 'in Christ Jesus'. So Paul also says:

> If we have been united with him like this in his death, we will certainly also be united with him in his resurrection. (Rom. 6:5)

It is this certainty which takes away from the believer the fear of death, a fear which afflicts many other people. What happens to them beyond death is a big question mark. For the Christian, there is no doubt. **His salvation is assured because of the amazing grace God has shown him.**

I have to fight feelings of jealousy when a believer is promoted to glory! What a comfort to know my turn will come at God's appointed time. Hallelujah!

RESURRECTION

Belief in the resurrection is vital to the whole Christian cause: 'And if Christ has not been raised, our preaching is useless and so is your faith' (1 Cor. 15:14). For if Jesus is not raised, we cannot be raised and therefore would not have salvation.

> But Christ has indeed been raised from the dead, the firstfruits of those who have fallen asleep. (v.20)

Christ is the firstfruits; then 'those who belong to him' (v.23) will be raised with Him. He must reign until He has put all His enemies under His feet. The last enemy to be destroyed is death.

Paul explains something of the nature of our resurrection and the difference between the natural and the risen body:

> The body that is sown is perishable, it is raised imperishable; it is sown in dishonour, it is raised in glory; it is sown in weakness, it is raised in power; it is sown a natural body, it is raised a spiritual body. (1 Cor. 15:42–44)

We shall bear the likeness of 'the man from heaven'. This final transformation will happen 'in a flash, in the twinkling of an eye, at the last trumpet' (v.52).

Meanwhile 'we, who with unveiled faces all reflect the Lord's glory, are being transformed into his likeness with an ever-increasing glory, which comes from the Lord, who is the Spirit' (2 Cor. 3:18).

The final transformation will take place when we see the Lord face to face; then we shall be like Him. This will be the glorious fulfilment of His purposes for us and every believer. We shall finally be like Him!

> May God himself, the God of peace, sanctify you through and through. May your whole spirit, soul and body be kept blameless at the coming of our Lord Jesus Christ. The one who calls you is faithful and he will do it. (1 Thess. 5:23–24)

So the Christian does not need to fear death. For him this is merely the gateway to the ultimate victory. For beyond death there is resurrection, a new risen body and glorious transformation into the likeness of Jesus.

THE FINAL VICTORY

God wants to heal His children of sickness that robs them of their health and effective witness as the children of His

Kingdom, that takes them prematurely from the ministries
He has for them now. But the believer is not afraid of going
to be with the Lord. He or she will join the great company
of the redeemed around God's throne:

> They are before the throne of God and serve him day and
> night in his temple; and he who sits on the throne will
> spread his tent over them. Never again will they hunger;
> never again will they thirst. The sun will not beat upon
> them, nor any scorching heat. For the Lamb at the centre
> of the throne will be their shepherd; he will lead them to
> springs of living water. And God will wipe away every
> tear from their eyes. (Rev. 7:15–17)

**Glory to God! You are among that number. How could you
ever doubt that you are called to personal victory? You have
the Lord's presence with you, His power within you and His
promise of eternal glory!**

Your key to a victorious life:
     WHEN YOU SEE THE LORD FACE TO FACE,
     YOU WILL BE LIKE HIM.

Appendix 1
Key Scriptures

1 Without faith it is impossible to please God. (Heb. 11:6)

2 The message of the cross is foolishness to those who are perishing, but to us who are being saved it is the power of God. (1 Cor. 1:18)

3 And whatever you do, whether in word or deed, do it all in the name of the Lord Jesus. (Col. 3:17)

4 The Spirit gives life; the flesh counts for nothing. (John 6:63)

5 The words I have spoken to you are spirit and they are life. (John 6:63)

6 Not everyone who says to me, 'Lord, Lord,' will enter the kingdom of heaven, but only he who does the will of my Father who is in heaven. (Matt. 7:21)

7 Be transformed by the renewing of your mind. Then you will be able to test and approve what God's will is – his good, pleasing and perfect will. (Rom. 12:2)

8 There is no fear in love. But perfect love drives out fear. (1 John 4:18)

9 If you hold to my teaching, you are really my disciples. Then you will know the truth, and the truth will set you free. (John 8:31–32)

10 Not as I will, but as you will. (Matt. 26:39)

11 Live by the Spirit, and you will not gratify the desires of the sinful nature. (Gal. 5:16)

12 God has poured out his love into our hearts by the Holy Spirit, whom he has given us. (Rom. 5:5)

13   I tell you the truth, my Father will give you whatever you ask in my name. (John 16:23)

14   The reason the Son of God appeared was to destroy the devil's work. (1 John 3:8)
I have given you authority . . . to overcome all the power of the enemy; nothing will harm you. (Luke 10:19)

15   Do not rejoice that the spirits submit to you, but rejoice that your names are written in heaven. (Luke 10:20)

16   Love your enemies, do good to those who hate you, bless those who curse you, pray for those who ill-treat you. (Luke 6:27–28)

17   No, in all these things we are more than conquerors through him who loved us. (Rom. 8:37)

18   In everything, do to others what you would have them do to you. (Matt. 7:12)

19   Do everything in love. (1 Cor. 16:14)

20   Give, and it will be given to you. A good measure, pressed down, shaken together and running over, will be poured into your lap. For with the measure you use, it will be measured to you. (Luke 6:38)

21   A man reaps what he sows. (Gal. 6:7)

22   Surely he took up our infirmities and carried our sorrows. (Isa. 53:4)

23   By his wounds we are healed. (Isa. 53:5)

24   It is for freedom that Christ has set us free. (Gal. 5:1)

25   I tell you the truth, if anyone keeps my word, he will never see death. (John 8:51)

26   Because he himself suffered when he was tempted, he is able to help those who are being tempted. (Heb. 2:18)

27   God opposes the proud but gives grace to the humble. (Prov. 3:34; Jas. 4:6; 1 Pet. 5:5)

28   I am the resurrection and the life . . . whoever lives and believes in me will never die. (John 11:25–26)

Appendix 2

Your Key to a Victorious Life

1 Faith in Jesus enables you to overcome.
2 All your needs have been met in the crucified Jesus.
3 The way of victory is to speak, act and pray in the name of Jesus.
4 Submit your soul (your mind, emotions and will) to the Holy Spirit.
5 Put God's word into practice.
6 Walk in obedience to Jesus.
7 Resist the negative thoughts which oppose faith; fill your mind with the positive truths of God's Word.
8 Do not allow your feelings to control you.
9 Believe what the Word tells you about yourself – not your own reason or feelings.
10 Willingly submit yourself to the authority of Jesus.
11 Consecrate your body to the Lord.
12 Set your heart on pleasing God.
13 Victorious prayer comes from a life of faith and obedience.
14 You have authority over the devil and all his works.
15 You have authority over demons because your name is written in heaven.
16 Your faith overcomes the world and all the ways you can be opposed.
17 Maintain a positive, faith attitude at all times.
18 Live with an attitude towards others of love, forgiveness and mercy.

19   Express your love for others in giving to them in practical ways.
20   Walk in faith, love and obedience and you will prosper.
21   Keep giving to the Lord and others.
22   Sickness will not triumph over you.
23   Resist sickness in the name of Jesus.
24   Christ has set you free to live in freedom.
25   Live by the truth of God's Word.
26   Walk in the Spirit; say 'No' to every temptation to indulge the flesh.
27   Walk humbly before God and others.
28   When you see the Lord face to face, you will be like Him.